BETTER CONNECTED

How Girls Are Using Social Media for Good

ORCA Think

*Question, connect and take action to become better citizens
with a brighter future. Now that's smart thinking!*

BETTER CONNECTED

How Girls Are Using Social Media for Good

Tanya Lloyd Kyi and Julia Kyi

illustrated by Vivian Rosas

ORCA BOOK PUBLISHERS

Published in Canada and the United States in 2022 by Orca Book Publishers.
orcabook.com

Library and Archives Canada Cataloguing in Publication
Title: Better connected : how girls are surviving and thriving online /
Tanya Lloyd Kyi and Julia Kyi ; illustrated by Vivian Rosas.
Names: Kyi, Tanya Lloyd, 1973- author. | Kyi, Julia, author. | Rosas, Vivian, illustrator.
Series: Orca think ; 5.
Description: Series statement: Orca think ; 5 | Includes bibliographical references and index.
Identifiers: Canadiana (print) 20210254904 | Canadiana (ebook) 20210254971 |
ISBN 9781459828575 (hardcover) | ISBN 9781459828582 (PDF) | ISBN 9781459828599 (EPUB)
Subjects: LCSH: Social media—Juvenile literature. | LCSH: Online social networks—Juvenile literature. |
LCSH: Girls—Social life and customs—Juvenile literature. |
LCSH: Internet and children—Juvenile literature. | LCSH: Internet and women—Juvenile literature.
Classification: LCC HQ784.I58 K95 2022 | DDC j302.23/1083—dc23

Library of Congress Control Number: 2021941163

Summary: Part of the nonfiction Orca Think series for middle-grade readers, this illustrated
book is an inspiring look at the positive and creative ways girls are using social media.

Orca Book Publishers is committed to reducing the consumption of nonrenewable resources in the
production of our books. We make every effort to use materials that support a sustainable future.

Orca Book Publishers gratefully acknowledges the support for its publishing programs provided
by the following agencies: the Government of Canada, the Canada Council for the Arts and the
Province of British Columbia through the BC Arts Council and the Book Publishing Tax Credit.

Cover and interior artwork by Vivian Rosas
Design by Rachel Page
Layout by Dahlia Yuen
Edited by Kirstie Hudson

Printed and bound in Canada.

25 24 23 22 • 1 2 3 4

To the girls who are redefining feminism, insisting on equity and forging new paths in the digital world. —T.K.

And for Adelaide and Aishwarya, the best co-leaders and friends. —J.K.

Contents

INTRODUCTION

Girls get a lot of grief about their online activities.

She's posting selfies? "That's so vain."

Signing petitions? "***Slacktivism***."

Texting friends? "She probably lacks real-life social skills."

And you may have seen media stories about the ways girls interact on sites such as Instagram and TikTok. Often the headlines read like this:

"Depression in Girls Linked to Higher Use of Social Media"

"Social Media Is Destroying the Lives of Teenage Girls"

"Half of Girls Are Bullied Online"

So, okay, the issues with social media are real. A recent study in Britain found that almost 40 percent of 14-year-old girls who spent five hours a day online showed symptoms of depression. Then there are the cases of girls being cyberbullied or shamed. Obviously the online world has dangers.

They *might* be texting their friends…or they might be planning world domination.
DANIEL M ERNST/SHUTTERSTOCK.COM

1

Julia   Tanya

#NoFilter

Julia: I wasn't even allowed to have Instagram until the ninth grade. And you only said yes—finally—because I was on student council, and the meetings were posted there.

Tanya: What kind of student council organizes on Instagram? Did you make that up?

Julia: No!

Tanya: Your dad's best friend is a high-school counselor, and he knew someone who got in trouble posting inappropriate photos of herself.

Julia: You're a professional researcher, and this is how you make your decisions? Because of Dad's best friend's student's cousin?

Tanya: Um…basically?

Julia: 🙁

But the headlines don't tell the whole story.

Girls are also using social media in creative, powerful ways. They're building diverse and supportive communities. They're claiming and reshaping spaces such as comic art and fandom. They're successfully changing the public conversation about subjects from gun control to body image.

We're a mom (Tanya) and daughter (Julia) from Vancouver, British Columbia. We've had to figure out our family rules for the online world, making a few detours along the way.

This is what we look like in real life, in the backyard, without the professional help of our illustrator or a filter!

As we surfed our social media feeds, from Twitter (Tanya) to Instagram (Julia), we noticed something. Despite the **trolls** and the self-esteem tolls, girls are using their platforms to change the world for the better. So while this book acknowledges the challenges, we're focusing on the less recognized—and more positive—parts of girls' online experiences.

Some people have used terms such as **hashtag feminism** or **fourth-wave feminism** to describe the ways young women are organizing and acting online. (More about this in chapter 1.) And in areas from environmental activism to **LGBT2Q+** rights, immigration policy to education access, girls are leading the way. They're showing up, teaming up and speaking up.

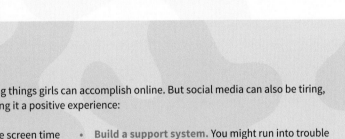

A few campaigners have earned international attention. In 2018 Greta Thunberg used Instagram to spearhead a global youth movement **IRL** (in real life). From the Amazon rainforest, Indigenous teen Helena Gualinga took to Instagram, Facebook and Twitter to reach like-minded climate protectors. And Bana Alabed was only eight years old when she used Twitter to show the world what it felt like to live through the siege of Aleppo. You'll read about all of these girls in the pages to come.

Better Connected is a celebration of achievement and leadership. We hope these stories give you an insider's look at the experiences of girls online. And who knows? Maybe they'll inspire you to create some world-changing waves of your own.

SOCIAL MEDIA SMARTS

In this book you'll read about the amazing things girls can accomplish online. But social media can also be tiring, scary or sad. Here are some tips for making it a positive experience:

- **Everything in moderation.** Make sure screen time isn't your whole life. Set a limit for the amount of time you'll spend online. And be sure to do other things you love, like playing sports or creating crafts. If you're new to social media, set up a plan with your parents and consider starting with 30 minutes a day.

- **Find your favorites.** There are so many platforms available. When you join your first one, take a few days to watch, read and learn. Then decide if that community is right for you. If you don't feel comfortable, check out a different site instead.

- **Build a support system.** You might run into trouble or bullies online, so know in advance who you'll talk to if that happens! Make a list of friends and trusted adults, such as teachers, parents or counselors.

- **Help create positive spaces.** Don't post mean comments or boost cruel videos. Follow people who make you happy and who make you feel good about yourself. Draw positivity from social media, and put positivity back in.

One
BUILDING BONDS
Creating Community Online

Maybe you arrange your books in rainbows on the floor. Maybe you create steampunk superhero costumes. Maybe you collect tiny unicorns, write historical zombie romances or game until 3:00 a.m. If so, there's an online community for you! In fact, there seems to be a digital space for every possible kind of girl.

Across websites, apps and platforms, young women have found countless ways to connect. For some, this kind of online sharing is a fun and creative pastime. For others—those who've moved around the world, for example, or those living with medical conditions—digital bonds act as lifelines.

This chapter is about young leaders who are passion-driven to build and sustain social media communities. Prepare to meet the most dedicated bloggers, the most popular Insta-influencers and everyone else in between.

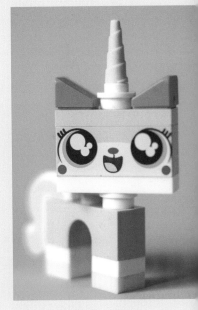

If this is your secret obsession, we're not judging.
HELLO I'M NIK/UNSPLASH.COM

In the 1970s and '80s, poet and activist Audre Lorde drew attention to the ways racism and sexism are connected.
ELSA DORFMAN/WIKIMEDIA COMMONS/ CC BY-SA 3.0

THE FOURTH WAVE

Fight for equal pay and social justice, all while sitting on your couch?

Sure. Why not?

The history of **feminism** is often described as a series of waves. During the first wave, in the 1800s and early 1900s, women fought for the rights to vote and own property. In the 1960s the second wave began. Women demanded workplace equality and reproductive rights. Then, in the third wave of the 1990s, women looked for things such as equal pay and an end to violence against women.

Jessica Valenti is the founder of the blog *Feministing*. In 2009 she suggested that maybe the fourth wave would be online. And over the years that followed, her prediction came true. Women and girls began taking their stories and their activism to the internet. Now fourth-wave feminism is thriving, as women speak out online about topics such as **intersectional feminism** and **body positivity**. (More about these in chapter 3.)

Julie Zeilinger is a part of this new wave. She was working on an eighth-grade assignment when she learned about something called *infanticide*. In parts of the world, male children are valued so much more than female that parents sometimes kill their own newborn girls.

Julie was horrified. How could this happen without ordinary people like her knowing about it? What other dangers were girls facing? She dove into research. She learned about feminism and **misogyny**. In high school Julie met a teacher who shared her ideals and helped her find books and resources.

In 2009, when she was 16, Julie founded her own blog. She loved the other feminist blogs she'd seen online, like *Feministing*, but she wanted a community specifically for

Today Julie Zeilinger is a freelance writer. She continues to focus on feminist issues.
JULIE ZEILINGER

young people. *The FBomb* was born—a feminist blog by teens and for teens. The site gathered 35,000 viewers in its first year. Working after school and on weekends, Julie set about building a true online community. She invited guest authors to post. She moderated and replied to comments from other teens. She continued writing her own posts, and she reached out to readers on social media channels.

Today *The FBomb* is part of the Women's Media Center, an organization founded by feminist powerhouses Jane Fonda, Robin Morgan and Gloria Steinem. But the blog remains a place for young people. It describes itself as "loud, proud, sarcastic and passionate—everything young feminists are today."

It's just one of the online communities where readers gather for a girl-power boost. Reddit, a giant online discussion forum, has a feminism page with thousands of members. Discord, a chat platform often used by gamers, has moderated spaces for young feminists. And Facebook has groups of girls discussing everything from classroom equality to abortion.

Julia's Headspace

With social media at our fingertips, standing up for girls and women has never been simpler. If there's a feminist issue you want to tackle, there's a group waiting for you. (And if by some small chance there isn't, you can create one with just a few clicks!)

The feminist movement isn't always well covered in school curriculums. But there's plenty of inspiring information online.

AJ_WATT/GETTY IMAGES

OPENING DIGITAL DOORS

Some girls, like Julie Zeilinger, want to build platforms that appeal to thousands or even millions. They want their groups to embrace as many people as possible. But other girls want more contained, controlled communities—and that's okay too!

When girls form a small Facebook homework club or Discord group chat, they're creating what's called—in official researcher terms—a *closed community*. A closed community is less like having a street party and more like gathering in a secret tree house with your friends. Small groups might include only people who know each other in real life. In larger closed communities, an administrator or moderator usually controls who can enter and watches for inappropriate content.

Just because a community is closed doesn't mean it's quiet. Some of these groups have major real-life effects.

In 2007 the National Center for Women & Information Technology (NCWIT) in the United States began giving computer-science awards to girls. The organization knew that only a tiny minority of programmers were female. They wanted to provide encouragement and support for girls considering computer-science careers.

In 2009 NCWIT launched a closed Facebook group and invited all previous award winners to join. For a few years membership was small and comments were rare. But as the awards continued, the chat grew more active. Soon members were sharing college recommendations and scholarship advice. And they were comparing notes—*a lot* of notes—about **sexism** in their field.

Obviously the community offered an emotional-support system. But did it have any effects on the lives of these girls and women? Professor Wendy DuBow from the University of Colorado Boulder decided to find out. She collected and analyzed the group's conversations between 2011 and 2015.

She concluded the group was political.

But the members weren't talking about votes or polls. So how could a Facebook group of computer scientists be political?

Many of the girls and women were mainly learning or working with men. Many of them experienced open sexism or **systemic bias**. Often they felt alone in their experiences. But thanks to the Facebook group, they realized that girls across the country were experiencing the same things. With the support of their virtual friends and mentors, girls found the strength and the strategies necessary to push back against **stereotypes**.

"It is political because it challenges the status quo," Wendy wrote in her research paper.

Through the words and actions of girls and women like these, discussions of systemic discrimination move from chat groups into real-life offices. They lead to meaningful

SOCIAL MEDIA SMARTS

Don't give out personal information on the internet. Don't give out personal information on the internet. If you're like Julia, you've heard it a million times. But what exactly counts as personal?

- **Intimate photos**. Obviously.

- **Passwords**. Again, pretty obvious.

- **Your phone number**. Because *a lot* of people online aren't exactly who they seem to be, and you wouldn't be the first smart, internet-savvy user to be tricked.

- **Your address**. This includes photos of the front of your house or identifiable views from your windows.

- **Your schedule**. *Can't wait to go away for the next seven days!* is like posting a sign saying, *Dear burglars, my house is empty.* And if you mention that you're heading for a specific coffee shop, stalkers—people who might follow and harass you— know exactly where to look.

Stay safe out there!

change in schools and workplaces. Eventually the systems themselves will start to change.

Even a closed community can influence the world.

OPEN UP!

It's time for the Universal Conglomeration of Pets to announce its Animal of the Year Award. And the prize goes to...dogs! Cue streamers! Cue confetti!

What's that, hamsters?

This is the 100th year in a row the prize has gone to dogs?

Well, try to grow a bit taller, and maybe you'll reach the podium next year.

Does something seem unfair in this scenario?

Systemic bias is prejudice shown by a large organization against a specific group. Worrying about dogs having more **privilege** than hamsters might seem silly. But when men are rewarded over women, or white people over Black people, those are serious forms of oppression.

What if your teacher assigns a research project, but some kids don't have computers at home? Can you think of ways to address this sort of inequity?

SDI PRODUCTIONS/GETTY IMAGES

This happens in governments, businesses and organizations. And it happens *all the time*. For example, if all the people on an interview panel are male, they're more likely to hire male employees...and the cycle continues.

But it doesn't have to happen in our online communities. If you're ever starting a group of your own, there are things you can do to make your space inclusive and welcoming:

- Set clear policies for respectful dialogue.
- Invite people from different backgrounds and ethnicities.
- Say hello, make introductions, and focus on personal connections.

Remember fourth grade, when your teacher chose you to show the new student around the school? Be that tour guide in online form!

GAMING THE SYSTEM

When girls introduce themselves as gamers, they often hear the same response:

"Oh...you don't look like one."

Though girls now make up about half of all video-game players, they still battle stereotypes. They have few girl avatars to choose from, they receive sexist messages from trolls, and they sometimes face serious sexual harassment. In competitive tournaments, they're often (mistakenly!) seen as easy prey, and they have to work harder to find sponsors.

None of this has stopped them.

Singapore gamer Tammy Tang (known online as furryfish) began playing as a kid. Her dad worked in technology, and a friend introduced her to *World of Warcraft* when she was still in elementary school. Now Tammy runs a competitive gaming team and organizes major conventions and tournaments.

This girl has a message we all need to hear.
DOUG MCLEAN/SHUTTERSTOCK.COM

Julia's Headspace

Why do video-game characters wear bikini tops while they walk through forests? They're going to have so many scratches! Seriously, though, there are too many female characters designed to appeal to men. Hopefully, as more women take leadership roles in the industry, we'll see a decrease in bizarre outfits and sexualization. And we'll see an increase in fun, creative and cooperative gaming.

Only a quarter of game designers identify as female, but today's girls might grow up to change those statistics.
OHISHIISTK/GETTY IMAGES

She credits live-streaming applications with bringing female gamers into the spotlight. Twitch, YouTube and Facebook allow girls to gain followers, build their reputations and eventually earn money through ad revenue, subscriptions and sponsorships.

The discussion of gender and gaming is complicated. Some girls would rather be seen simply as gamers rather than girl gamers. Others play male characters online. (And plenty of males play female characters online.) Many game designers still cast men in the leading roles and women as damsels in distress, and plenty of multiplayer games have serious problems with sexism and misogyny within their communities.

Research suggests that there's a disconnect. There are lots of females playing, but not many great female characters. It seems as if the industry has some catching up to do.

CROSS-BORDER CONNECTING

Some refugee organizations run tablet-lending services to help new arrivals contact their families, build connections in their new cities and access virtual learning opportunities.

MASKOT/GETTY IMAGES

Wanted: new friend to act as language coach, tutor, confidant, counselor, comedian and tour guide. Expertise in multiple subjects and cultures required.

Can you imagine this as a Craigslist ad? You'd never find one person to fill the role. And yet this "person" is exactly who refugees need when they arrive in a new country.

In 2015, after millions of Syrians were displaced by war, the Canadian government embarked on a massive resettlement project. In just over a year, almost 40,000 Syrians arrived to begin new lives. About half of them were children. After surviving a war and long months in refugee camps, they were suddenly expected to learn English or French, fit into their new schools and—in their spare time—deal with years of emotional trauma.

Fortunately they had a tool that refugees and immigrants of previous generations didn't have—social media.

Three researchers at the University of Ottawa set out to learn how that tool might help. They recruited 29 volunteers, ages 16 to 25. Some had been in Canada for almost a year. One had arrived only 13 days before the study began.

The researchers wanted to know how new arrivals used social media.

They found that many worked on their language skills by watching videos in English and French on Facebook, Instagram, WhatsApp and YouTube. Others read Arabic news streams about Canadian culture, looking for tips on how to adjust and fit in.

As the young people made friends who were born in Canada, the feeds of those friends offered even more hints and tips about life in the new country. (In one case, a new arrival asked, "What is this tree of Christmas?") The cultural exchanges went both ways, as the new arrivals created content about their own traditions and shared posts and photos with Canadian-born friends.

There were practical social media uses too. One study participant gathered tips on how to buy a car. Another looked for college course recommendations.

In their writing, the researchers called social media a "borderland"—a place between cultures. People can find friends at their new school through Instagram or contact family back home over WhatsApp. For young people in the process of adapting to a new culture, social media offers both a link to past communities and a bridge to new ones.

Want to start your own media empire? Many public libraries now offer space where you can record podcasts, film and edit videos, or publish ebooks.

JASMIN MERDAN/GETTY IMAGES

CLICK LIT

You're reluctant to turn the final page. You've fallen in love with the characters, and you don't want the book to end...

If you've ever felt that way, you're not alone. That's part of the reason fan fiction has boomed in popularity. Fan fiction is writing inspired by a previous published work. It's a way for fans to further develop their favorite characters, relationships and worlds. And while the literary snobs out there might not regard it as serious writing, it's sparked huge communities of creators and readers.

Beth Reekles began reading fan fiction and other work on Wattpad when she was a young teen. The platform allows anyone to write and publish their own stories. It also has a messaging system, so authors and readers can communicate. It's home to thousands of fandoms, from One Direction "Directioners" to Percy Jackson "Demigods." Wattpad has even launched its own publishing company, making traditional print books and audiobooks.

When Beth was 15, she began posting her own stories. One of her creations, *The Kissing Booth,* won Wattpad's Teen Fiction award. Soon traditional book publishers came knocking at Beth's (virtual) door. After she accepted a publishing deal, her online stories grew into print books, then became a series of wildly successful Netflix movies. And the supportive community vibe of fan fiction continues. Today there are pages and pages of Wattpad fan fiction written in honor of Beth's work!

#No Filter

Julia: I'm impressed by the story behind *The Kissing Booth*, but...

Tanya: Not your favorite?

Julia: The author is inspiring, the marketing was great, the story was...a cheesefest.

Tanya: I never mind a little cheese with my romance, personally.

COMIC SUPERPOWERS

What if you had the power to erase memories? What if you hunted supernatural beings or traveled through time?

Online comics allow artists to bring their ideas to life, no matter how serious or how silly. There are thousands of independent artists creating everything from superhero sagas to pop-music-themed mysteries. Traditionally comics are a male-dominated genre. But women are breaking through, especially on online platforms.

Famous for her anime-inspired style, Vancouver Island artist Camilla d'Errico has created coloring books, classes and comics. In an interview with *Bust Magazine*, she emphasized the importance of females in comics: "I think women have a lot to say in comics and art." She said she makes softer, more emotional pieces in hopes of creating safe spaces at conventions for people to enjoy atypical comics. She once called her comic-con booth "a candy store in the middle of a metal show." And Camilla's many female fans certainly appreciate her focus on girls, nature and creativity.

Social media and the internet offer all sorts of new mediums and publishing opportunities. There are girls and women expressing themselves in genres from horror to comedy. And often, as in fan fiction, those audiences become powerful communities of like-minded people.

RARE CONNECTIONS

Florida resident Claire Barrow lost two teeth when she was only a year old. A few years later she broke a bone in her hand while playing with a string—a string! Obviously, something was wrong. But Claire's mom took her to countless doctors. No one could offer a diagnosis.

Finally, when she was 12, Claire saw a specialist who provided a name for her disorder: hypophosphatasia. It's a rare genetic condition that affects the development of bones and teeth. Claire's mom and grandmother tested positive for the condition as well.

It was a relief to have a diagnosis. But Claire still felt alone in the world. She couldn't find any kids in her area who shared her condition.

She knew there must be other girls in other parts of the world who were also searching for diagnoses or community support. So, with her mom's help, Claire created an app called RareGuru. She launched it in 2020, when she was 13. The app offers a way to connect patients and caregivers. Users list their diagnosis or their symptoms and receive connection requests from people with similar conditions.

Claire's not alone in turning to social media to find people with rare disorders. Dr. Kurt Schumacher is a children's heart specialist at a hospital in Michigan. He knew it was often difficult to study rare disorders because it was hard to find enough patients to participate. But he'd also noticed that he and his colleagues were using a new tool—the internet. He set out to find patients to participate in a study of two rare conditions, a digestive disorder and a lung disease, and to track how social media worked as a referral source.

Here's what Kurt wrote in his 2014 research paper: "Patients who have similar diseases cluster 'virtually' online

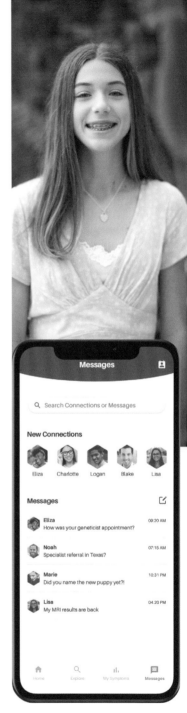

Claire Barrow's RareGuru app has a user group specifically for teens, so they can connect with other young people.

RAREGURU, LLC

via social media." By posting his research needs on his website and on Facebook for a year, Kurt found 124 people with the conditions. And 84 percent of the patients had learned about him through Facebook, internet forums or websites.

When people like Claire create communities (or clusters, as Kurt called them), they're not only building support groups for themselves. They're also building pools of potential subjects for research projects. They're helping the researchers who will eventually—hopefully!—help cure their disorders.

In the United States, a disease is officially considered rare when it affects fewer than 1 in 200,000 people. The category includes many genetic disorders and childhood cancers.

EUJARIMPHOTOGRAPHY/GETTY IMAGES

If you're the administrator of an online forum, make sure you show any inappropriate posts to a trusted adult.

SOCIAL MEDIA SMARTS

Creating your own forum for unicorn believers? Or maybe you're already an active member of a robot-building bootcamp. Here are a few suggestions for keeping your community strong:

- **Report abuse**. Whether a troll is targeting you or you see someone else getting cyberbullied, let the administrators know ASAP. Everyone in your community should feel safe to speak and share—respectfully.

- **Protect the personal**. Remind participants not to share their addresses, phone numbers or passwords.

- **Bite your electronic tongue**. Sometimes people are annoying. But before you fly off the handle, ask yourself what your response will accomplish. Will it be helpful to the community? Are you open to advice or solutions? Are you helping create a positive space? If you're simply venting your negative vibes, try a diary instead.

- **Click with care**. Everything lives forever on the internet. Even if you're in a closed community, people can save or screenshot your posts. As always, think twice and post once—and encourage others to do the same.

Two
IMAGINATION ON THE INTERNET

Expressing Creativity Online

Have you ever created a picture from punctuation marks? Told a story in emojis? Used filters to transform your beach selfie into an otherworldly scene? There are thousands of ways to get imaginative online. Much of the fun and novelty of social media comes from discovering other people's innovations and posting our own.

Some girls have discovered ways to combine vision, talent and the reach of the internet to do even more, establishing themselves as artists or turning their passion projects into business ventures. This chapter celebrates the girls who paint bold creations on a social media canvas, from filmmakers and makeup moguls to jingle dancers and calligraphers.

THE BIG BREAK

Maybe Grandma's strawberry shortcake won a blue ribbon. Maybe Great-Aunt Loretta's quilts still decorate your house. Fifty or a hundred years ago, women's creative projects were

A TikTok account with a rock-climbing theme? Yes, please!
TREVOR WILLIAMS/GETTY IMAGES

Social media sites allow girls to learn, create and share their guitar solos, their spoken word or their fashion creations.

often meant only for home and family—and sometimes for the judges at the fall fair.

Today that's all changed. The internet offers opportunities for instant fame and recognition, and plenty of **Gen Z** celebrities established their fan bases by sharing their creative talents online.

You might not think "political activist" when you see a fashion model. But Amelie Zilber juggles both identities. She got her start as a young teen, posting fashion and modeling shots on Instagram. She was quickly signed by LA Model Management, and her dance videos on TikTok earned her even more fans.

Then Amelie decided to use her platform for change.

She founded *TwoMinuteTimes*, a site that posts news stories each week about climate change, the refugee crisis and other social justice issues. Its tagline is "knowledge = power." Amelie also works as a youth ambassador for UNICEF and as a columnist for American journalist Maria Shriver.

Amelie used her creative talents to build a fan base, parlayed that fan base into a modeling career, then used her international platform to pursue her passion for social justice. That's a lot to accomplish while still a teen.

Around the world millions of other girls are using social media to pursue their passions. They exchange craft ideas on Pinterest, sell paintings on Etsy or aesthetically arrange their #bookstagram materials. Arabic social media star Njoud Al Shammari has connected with millions of fans and followers through her lifestyle and makeup channel. From her home in Saudi Arabia, Njoud posts YouTube videos about everything from applying mascara to manicure styles. Her audience peaks during Ramadan, the Muslim month of fasting and prayer, when she shares preparation techniques, beauty tips and recipes for post-sunset feasts. Not many girls in Saudi Arabia run their own media platforms. But soon after launching her channel, Njoud became the country's first female creator to draw more than a million followers.

For some girls, like Njoud and Amelie, the internet offers a "big break" and international fame. For others, it's simply a place to get creative and to share work with like-minded people. Either way, social media gives girls access to audiences that women of previous generations could never have imagined.

PASSION PROJECTS

Not every creative teen scores a record label or a movie deal. But maybe not everyone needs to. Recently online success stories have prompted questions about the traditional commercial world of art. What does it mean to be a professional creator? Do you need a paycheck to be successful? Or can you call yourself an artist if you share your work, receive feedback from others and strive to improve, whether or not you get rich?

Researchers and pop-culture experts are wrestling with these questions. One possible answer is that creativity has

#NoFilter

Tanya: Ever since you stole access to my Pinterest account, it's full of pasta recipes and skirt patterns.

Julia: I know! Isn't it perfect?

Tanya:
I have to admit, you are the all-time ruler of using social media creatively. Selling collage kits, finding Irish pen pals, learning spoken word, trading used clothing…

Julia: You use Twitter and Facebook to share creative things.

Tanya: Mostly I use them to make sure the apocalypse hasn't happened while I've been writing.

Julia: Yes, but you're *creatively* monitoring for the apocalypse.

Tanya: Sure. And I like those little videos about how to make soup in only five steps…

Julia: See? There's hope for you.

The metal cones on a jingle dress are called *ziibaaska'iganan* in the Ojibwe language.

uses that extend far beyond winning awards and making money.

In 2020, during the COVID-19 pandemic, 11-year-old Shyla Tootoosis from Thunderchild First Nation in Saskatchewan was one of hundreds of girls to post a video of herself in a jingle dress, performing a traditional dance and prayer. A jingle dress is exactly what it sounds like—a garment embellished with tiny metal cones that jingle with every movement. It's meant to be worn while performing "a really beautiful dance that provides healing," as Shyla described it to Canada's CBC News.

"When I was growing up, I was always taught to pray for one another," she said. "And it was a true honor to pray for the world."

Before the pandemic, few people had heard of jingle dancing. Then suddenly millions of viewers were watching dancers from tiny communities in Manitoba, Wyoming and North Dakota. No one grew rich from the girls' creativity. But for many viewers, the dances offered hope and light during a frightening time.

CLICK HAPPY

A hooded teen stares, eyes glazed, into her phone. A girl with ripped jeans and chipped nail polish sits on a city curb, scrolling through her texts. A third girl sprawls on her bed, reading messages from a cyberbully. These are the types of images that appear in news articles about teens and technology.

In 2019 researchers at the University of Bern in Switzerland combed through the files of major stock-photography companies—the firms that supply photos to the world's news outlets. They chose the top 600 hits for "teens and technology." Then they analyzed the headlines of the media stories that had used those images.

What they found was depressing. And misleading.

The most common news topics were technology addiction, teens' deteriorating communication skills, miscommunication, social disconnection, *sexting*, sleep issues and mental illness. The photos alongside these articles were disembodied fingers on keyboards, or generic teen girls staring at their screens.

What do you think? Does this stock photo reflect your real-life experiences?
ANTONIO GUILLEM/SHUTTERSTOCK.COM

SOCIAL MEDIA SMARTS

Selfies aren't all vain and vapid. They can be fun, and many girls call them confidence boosters. If you're planning to embark on a selfie spree, here are few safety guidelines:

- **Don't scare Grandma.**
  Never post anything that would shock your grandma—or your future boss.

- **Keep it clean.**
  The knife might be a plastic prop and the beer bottle might be empty, but do you really want to explain that to your parents? Or your principal?

- **Pick your places.**
  No funeral homes, no selfies out the car window, and definitely no clifftops.

The researchers argue that the photo banks and news outlets are skewing teens' online activities in three ways:

- by repeatedly using generic photos
- by ignoring the diversity of teens' social communications
- by using vague images to imply negative themes

Are all teens addicted to technology, losing their social skills and experiencing mental illness? Of course not! In fact, some are designing apps to bring people together.

In junior high school, one of Ariana (Ari) Sokolov's friends was struggling with her bisexual identity and how to share it. After thinking about her friend's plight and researching the issues around LGBT2Q+ youth and mental health, 16-year-old Ari created The Trill Project, an app and social network, to offer support. The California coder quickly gained international attention. Her app was downloaded 50,000 times in 41 countries and featured as Apple's App of the Day. Today her app has more than 75,000 users.

The stock photograph for Ari's app-creation experience would be a far more positive image than most!

Ari Sokolov's app uses special software to ensure that its users remain anonymous.

THE TRILL PROJECT

Girl coders say their fellow females simply don't realize how collaborative and creative coding can be. Fortunately there are role models changing the way the world sees STEM (science, technology, engineering and math).

One of these role models is a former *Tonight Show* guest, a Google prize winner and an inventor. Canadian Filipino student Ann Makosinski was 15 when she won her age category at a Google science fair in 2013. Her project was inspired by a friend in the Philippines who was struggling in school—without electricity, she didn't have enough light to study by at night. Ann came to the rescue with a flashlight powered by the heat of the user's hand. Along the way, she won tens of thousands of dollars in prize money and scholarships.

Ann has given three TEDx talks, and she shares messages about STEM and positivity with her nearly 21,000 Instagram followers. In an interview with *Glamour Magazine*, she summed up her philosophy this way: "It's important to tell kids that the arts and sciences can work together, instead of telling them, 'Science is a career, and arts is a hobby.' I use both in my work."

In 2015 Ann created a phone-charging mug. And she has lots of ideas for medical innovations in the future.

Like Ann, Heidi Wang believes girls in STEM can change the world for the better. After she earned her computer-science degree, she began an internship at a software-engineering company. When she went to her first meeting, she was the only woman in the room.

Heidi started thinking about the stereotypes she'd encountered as a girl, and how other girls might overcome them too. She also thought about all the inspiring ways her female friends were using their coding skills. Couldn't more girls learn to do the same?

Ann Makosinski is a tech innovator, but she uses a flip phone! Check out her TEDx talk online to find out why.
FLICKR.COM/KALOIAN/MINISTERIO DE CULTURA DE LA NACIÓN/CC BY-SA 2.0

Heidi won a grant from an online contest, and Girls Teaching Girls to Code was born. The organization runs interactive workshops, special events and an annual summer camp at Stanford University in California. By providing female mentors and offering a wide range of coding challenges in a fun and creative atmosphere, Heidi and her colleagues hope to close the gender gap in computer science, once and for all.

MIX AND MATCH

In the 1600s Europe's coffeehouses were places where rich people sat beside poor people, exchanging ideas and swapping newspapers. Traders talked to musicians. Mapmakers talked to playwrights. Isaac Newton once dissected a dolphin on a coffee-shop table. (Yuck, but you get the idea.) Many people think these coffeehouse exchanges helped lead to the Age of Enlightenment, a period in the 17th and 18th centuries when reason, art and science were celebrated.

Do you notice any similarities between 17th-century coffeehouses and social media? Okay, social media might not *always* be a celebration of reason (ahem, baby-goat videos), but it *is* a place to exchange ideas with masses of other people from all over the world, who are working in all sorts of mediums. Who knows what new Age of Enlightenment we could create?

In 17th-century Paris, messengers carried thousands of notes across the city each day. Today we use TikTok and Twitter instead.

(L) PHYNART STUDIO/GETTY IMAGES / (R) SIX_CHARACTERS/GETTY IMAGES

Let your parents know that you're posting your talents online. Then put Mom to work as camera operators!

SOCIAL MEDIA SMARTS

Feel like taking your creative talents online? Here are a few things to consider.

- **Safety**. As you're choosing a platform, read its policies. How is the community monitored? Check sites such as Common Sense Media for safety tips. And keep your parents in the loop.

- **Privacy**. Study up on how to keep your public life and your private life separate. You'll want to avoid mentioning your phone number or address, of course, and keep those things out of photos and videos. Feel free to block and report users who seem a little too interested in your personal life. (For more privacy tips, flip back to chapter 1.)

- **Ownership**. You're posting your talents, but you're not giving them away. So make sure your social media platforms let you keep the rights to your work.

Three
DIGITAL DIVERSITY
Making Space Online...for Everyone!

"Hey! Over here! Pay attention to me!"

For People of Color, girls, LGBT2Q+ people and many others, drawing attention to an issue or an injustice can feel like shouting into a void.

Traditionally media outlets have hired mostly white, *cis* men. Only 25 percent of American evening-news hosts are women. At daily newspapers, only 13 percent of journalists are People of Color. A research team at Canada's Simon Fraser University found that when journalists quoted sources, about 75 percent of those sources were male.

Thank goodness for social media! While there's still a gender gap in internet users, it's much, much smaller than in any other media source. And social media lets anyone share ideas and draw followers without trying to flag down a news anchor.

Julia's Headspace

Cis is a short form of *cisgender* (pronounced "sis-gender"), and it describes someone whose gender identity is the same as it was described at birth. It recognizes that gender isn't something we should assume.

In this chapter, we'll explore how girls and teens are telling their own stories, making space for people who are underrepresented, and creating online worlds...worlds of unprecedented diversity.

THE TANGLED OCTOPUS

How is discrimination like an octopus? Well, for many people, it's a many-tentacled thing!

In chapter 1 we talked about feminist communities. But over the past few decades, people have realized that feminism is more complicated than holding a Girl Power sign. Imagine an octopus with a different issue on each tentacle—**homophobia**, **transphobia**, sexism, racism, etc. If you're a girl, you're dealing with sexism. But if you're a girl, a person of color and LGBT2Q+, you're dealing with a lot of tangled arms and suckers.

Author and speaker Mona Eltahawy was the first to describe intersectional feminism as an octopus. She was building on the work of Kimberlé Crenshaw, who coined the term *intersectionality* in a 1989 research paper. That word was initially meant to express the way Black women faced two kinds of oppression, sexism *and* racism. Now the idea is at the forefront of fourth-wave feminism. Intersectional feminists are advocates for all **marginalized groups**, not just women.

On social media, activists encourage users to consider different groups and amplify the voices of people who aren't always heard.

Imagine you're a rock star. You're rich, white and straight. Oh, and your dad's a music producer. So when someone asks you whether it's tough to get started in music, you might reply, "Nah, it's easy if you have talent."

Well, it was easy for *you*! You were born with all sorts of advantages. You have privilege.

So how would you answer in an ideal world? Well, your rock-star self might say, "I was lucky, but lots of talented people go unnoticed. Check out the work of these amazing up-and-coming musicians of color!"

There are many real-life stars who use their privilege in generous and uplifting ways. Visit the social media feeds of Andy Samberg (of *Brooklyn Nine-Nine* fame), Mark Ruffalo (also known as the Hulk) or musician Harry Styles to see feminism, environmentalism and anti-racism in action.

Singer-songwriter Sarah McLachlan has paid her success forward by funding the Sarah McLachlan School of Music, which provides free music education to inner-city kids.

A KATZ/SHUTTERSTOCK.COM

CANCEL CULTURE

When people act offensively on social media, they sometimes get **called out**. Tons of other users speak out against them. They earn a lot of bad publicity and can lose millions of followers, not to mention sponsorship deals.

This sort of group justice is often called *cancel culture.*

Some of these online actions can seem a bit silly. TikTok star Dixie D'Amelio was once canceled for not wanting to eat escargot. Critics called her "culturally insensitive." But her supporters said, "Hey, we know snails are a traditional French food. But they look gross. What's the big deal?"

While the debate raged on, Dixie lost thousands of followers.

Other times when someone is called out, it reveals real rifts in society. J.K. Rowling, beloved author of the Harry Potter series, posted a series of tweets questioning whether trans women should be considered women. Many of her former fans were quick to boycott her work.

Dixie D'Amelio (right) and her sister, Charli (left), rocketed to fame on TikTok in 2019.

MONICA SCHIPPER/GETTY IMAGES

#No Filter

Tanya: Your dad was born in Myanmar, and I'm white, which makes you a mix of the two. Do you get questions about your ethnicity?

Julia: Not really. Just "But where are you *from* from?"

Tanya: From from?

Julia: As in, "I know you're from Canada, but where are you really from?"

Tanya: Okay, that's offensive.

Julia: I get it. They're trying to figure me out. I don't look Chinese, Japanese or Korean, but I'm probably some sort of "other Asian."

Tanya: PEOPLE DON'T NEED TO BE CATEGORIZED!

She chose not to apologize. Instead she tried to justify her views. And that led to an even bigger backlash! Harry Potter film stars Daniel Radcliffe and Emma Watson publicly condemned her posts. She lost hundreds of thousands of social media followers, and her book sales reportedly plunged.

J.K. Rowling joined about 150 authors and professors who signed a letter in *Harper's Magazine*. They wrote that public shaming and boycotts threatened free speech and restricted the free exchange of information and ideas.

It's important to hold people accountable when they say racist, biased or derogatory things. It's important to stand up for the rights of marginalized people. But does cancel culture ever go too far? What do you think?

Intersectional feminists have certainly used the collective power of social media, call-outs and even cancel culture to change the conversation about feminism, power and privilege—online and in real life. And across social media, girls are speaking up about the intersections at which they stand.

This version of the transgender pride flag was created by American Monica Helms in 1999. Its stripes represent the spectrum of genders.

INK DROP/SHUTTERSTOCK.COM

쥬얼리성형외과
Plastic Surgery Center

수술실력으로 입증 된!
쥬얼리성형외과

ด้วยความสามารถ
ในการผ่าตัด
ที่ถูกพิสูจน์ให้เห็น
ผ่านผลพร้อมอย่างชัดเจน

BODIES OF EVIDENCE

Doubts about your body? Concerns that your nose is too round, your breasts are too small or your belly's too big? The internet is *not* the place to find reassurance!

By 2016 there were more than 20 studies showing a strong link between social media use and girls' dissatisfaction with their bodies. But did social media cause the self-esteem issues, or did girls with self-esteem issues simply gravitate toward social media? Which one created the other?

A group of Dutch scientists decided to figure it out. They surveyed 600 students about three main subjects:

- social media use
- the criticisms or compliments of their friends
- their feelings about their bodies

A little over a year later, the same teens were surveyed again. Here's what the researchers found. Frequent social media use predicted body dissatisfaction, for girls more than for boys. They also found that no matter how nice people's friends were—no matter how many times they said, "What are you talking about? You look *great* in that dress!"—social media still made teens doubt themselves.

But it's not all bad news. British researcher Amy Slater recruited 160 female college students. She showed some of them "fitspiration" photos of thin women exercising. She showed other students quotes about self-compassion. A third group viewed neutral, non-body-related images.

Companies spend more than US$7.5 billion a year advertising beauty and personal-care products. Is it any wonder women think they need more makeup or shinier hair?
(L) SORBIS/SHUTTERSTOCK.COM /
(R) HANANEKO_STUDIO/SHUTTERSTOCK.COM

Social comparison theory is an idea developed by psychologists in the 1950s. Today's research shows that comparing ourselves to others might motivate us to improve…or it might make us feel hopelessly inferior.
ROB HAINER/SHUTTERSTOCK.COM

In Amy's study, the women who read quotes about self-compassion felt better about their bodies, felt more compassionate toward themselves and were happier overall. And there are plenty of social media users who promote that sort of self-love.

When she was 14, Rianna Kish developed orthorexia, an obsession with healthy eating. In the next couple of years she was diagnosed with other eating disorders, all the while fighting anxiety and bipolar disorder. As a senior in high school, Rianna started a TikTok account about her eating-disorder recovery, hoping to use dance as a healthy coping mechanism. She is now a body-positive role model for over 300,000 followers as she works to create a safe space on social media. She's transparent about the ups and downs of recovery and tells her followers about self-love, honoring cravings, conquering "fear foods" and breaking societal binds. Rianna's goal is to show young girls like herself that they are more than their body or their weight. (Here's one of Rianna's questions for her followers: *What do you love most about yourself?*)

There are lots of other body-positive mentors on social media, from yoga instructors and disability advocates to celebrity chefs and actors—those such as Jameela Jamil. A former journalist, she rose to fame after playing Tahani on *The Good Place*. As an eating-disorder survivor, she's an outspoken advocate of body positivity, and she's called out other celebs for promoting unproven diet products. As a woman of color who also identifies as queer, Jameela is committed to using her platform to create change and make safe spaces for marginalized communities.

If you're ever finding the online "fitspiration" a little overwhelming, you're not alone. Try seeking out the body-positive posts instead.

Jameela Jamil's #iweigh campaign encourages people to look past appearances and instead share their accomplishments.

EYE OPENING

Happy 16th birthday, sweetheart! We've bought you just what you asked for—a nose job.

In South Korea, beauty standards are even more rigorous than they are in North America. Sixty percent of 20-year-old women in the capital city of Seoul have undergone some sort of plastic surgery—often skin-whitening procedures, nose jobs or double-eyelid surgeries intended to make eyes look more stereotypically Western.

But recently some girls have used social media to launch a full-scale rebellion against their beauty routines. Jeon Bora is a competitive judo athlete turned photographer. When she was 25, she captured dozens of portraits of South Korean girls and women as they shed their feminine clothing and shaved their heads as part of the country's Escape the Corset movement.

#NoFilter

Tanya: Makeup tutorials and feminism. Discuss.

Julia: Do you mean are they compatible? They can be. You don't have to wear makeup for other people. You can wear it as a form of expression.

Tanya: Hmmm...my form of expression in high school was blue eyeshadow, which I thoroughly regret.

Julia: I have no comment on this.

Of course, South Korean women aren't wearing actual corsets. But that remnant of Victorian-era fashion—the laced, whale-boned undergarment designed to make women appear thin—serves as a symbol of stereotyping and oppression.

Before 2018, YouTube star Lina Bae spent her time giving bronzer tutorials. But after reading comments from tweens and teens feeling pressure to be beautiful, Lina second-guessed her career. She shared a collection of the hateful comments she'd received about her looks, and she posted a video of herself removing her makeup, one layer at a time.

"It's okay not to be pretty," she told viewers.

With role models like Jeon and Lina, girls in South Korea (and around the world) are making a societal shift, online and in real life.

Self-love means treating yourself with the same kindness and respect you show your best friends and your family members.
ALEX LIEW/GETTY IMAGES

PEOPLE POLITICS

A few years ago University of Chicago professor Cathy Cohen and researcher Matthew Luttig teamed up to answer a big question. Could the internet provide a way for young people—especially young people from minority groups—to get involved in politics?

From previous research, they knew that people with money were much more likely to be politically active than poorer people. People with money were more likely to campaign, vote and protest. They were even more likely to watch the news.

But thanks to work by a group called the MacArthur Research Network on Youth and Participatory Politics, Cathy and Matthew discovered something. Young People of Color weren't watching the news, they were watching social media.

They were regularly visiting news sites designed by and for People of Color—sites such as *The Black Youth Project* and *presente.org*.

The researchers surveyed young internet users in 2013 and again in 2015. Over those two years, there were two groups that began talking more about politics on social media and engaging more with political issues—disadvantaged and **BIPOC** youth.

It turns out social media gives people from minority groups a stronger voice and even helps them take that voice off-line, into the real world.

PICTURE IMPERFECT

"Making space" for People of Color sometimes gets literal.

At a press conference held in Switzerland, Vanessa Nakate posed shoulder to shoulder for a photo with four other teen activists. Vanessa is the founder of Youth for Future Africa and the Rise Up Movement, and she'd traveled from her home in Uganda for a weekend of workshops and discussion panels.

But when the Associated Press (AP) posted its photo of the activists, Vanessa was missing. Only the edge of her jacket showed along one side of the shot. Greta Thunberg stood in the center of the image. Three other white activists were there. Only Vanessa had been cropped.

A generation before, someone in Vanessa's situation would have been left powerless. She could have written a letter to the editor and maybe received a tiny apology in the corner of the next newspaper issue. But Vanessa had tens of thousands of social media followers.

Inspired by Greta Thunberg, Vanessa Nakate started her own climate strike outside the Parliament of Uganda in 2019.

PAUL WAMALA SSEGUJJA/WIKIMEDIA COMMONS/CC BY-SA 4.0

She tweeted the AP. *Why did you remove me from the photo? I was part of the group!*

Immediately other activists leaped into action, tweeting, writing blog posts and speaking to media outlets. To many, the photo cropping seemed like a symbol of the way People of Color are left out of the conversation even though they're the ones most directly affected by climate change.

Less wealthy countries like Uganda have fewer resources to help their people cope with droughts or storms. In North America, People of Color have lower average incomes than white people. They have less access to healthcare and other resources. So they're more susceptible too. One California study found that heat waves are more likely to kill Black babies than white. (A major factor is that wealthier people have better air-conditioning.) There are plenty of reasons for People of Color to take action on climate change. And yet they're not often heard.

"Climate activists of color are erased," Vanessa told Britain's *Guardian* newspaper.

The AP apologized, saying the crop was a simple mistake with no racial bias intended. And maybe the photo crop *was* entirely accidental. Maybe it was a sign of implicit bias—an editor with subconscious prejudice. Or maybe it was intentional. We'll never know. But Vanessa's experience shows why it can be more difficult for People of Color to show up, speak out and be heard. Fortunately for Vanessa, her followers sprang to her defense.

Singer-songwriter Ta'Kaiya Blaney from the Tla'Amin First Nation in British Columbia is a young activist calling for governments to address the issues of environmental justice and the rights of Indigenous Peoples.

MICHAEL WHEATLEY/ALAMY STOCK PHOTO

TRUE COLORS

"I can't breathe."

On May 25, 2020, George Floyd, a Black man in Minneapolis, Minnesota, was stopped on the street by police. They said he'd used counterfeit money to buy cigarettes. Police officer Derek Chauvin knelt on George's neck for nine minutes, while George pleaded for his life.

George died, unable to breathe.

Protests erupted across the United States and around the world. Activists spoke out against police violence against Black people and about the wider issue of systemic racism, a type of racism so ingrained in our systems and societies that we often fail to recognize it.

To Lauren Gloster, a student at a New York private school, the situation seemed all too familiar. George's death

True Colors of Columbia offers a space for students of color to share their stories in their own words.

TRUE COLORS OF COLUMBIA

The Black Lives Matter movement was born in 2013, following the acquittal of the man who killed 17-year-old Trayvon Martin in Florida.

MICHAL URBANEK/SHUTTERSTOCK.COM

was the latest in a long list, and Lauren saw more subtle forms of discrimination all around her. But she knew that many students felt powerless to speak up. Some were on scholarships and didn't want to jeopardize their funding. Others were scared. A few had been assaulted, and one had been threatened with **lynching**.

Lauren decided to create a space where students could have a voice while still protecting their identities—and their scholarships. She launched True Colors of Columbia, an Instagram account where students could post about their experiences. Soon hers was one of about 60 similar accounts exposing injustices at schools across the country.

Some students wrote about **microaggressions**—people saying inappropriate things, or teachers marking them unfairly. Others wrote about more extreme threats and assaults.

"It's really difficult to learn in an environment where you don't feel safe every day," Lauren told news reporters. "One of the biggest issues is that students of color feel like they can't vocalize their injustice."

But Lauren's Instagram account, and others like hers, gave those students a platform. She and other student representatives asked American schools for changes:

· more Black history in the curriculum
· more People of Color on faculty
· repercussions for racism in the classroom

A spokesperson from Lauren's school told ABC News: "It is clear that we have important and long-overdue work ahead. We are ready and committed."

Lauren isn't the only girl using the internet to fight racism—or the youngest. After kids in her first-grade class made fun of her dark skin, Kheris Rogers tried taking extra-long baths, hoping to lighten her complexion. But her mom and her older sister helped her find a new way of seeing her skin color. (And find a different school!)

At age 10, Kheris launched her own clothing line on social media. Her clothes bore slogans such as "Flexin' in My Complexion" and "The Miseducation of Melanin." By the time she was 12, she'd worked with stars such as LeBron James and Tyra Banks, and had been featured on *Teen Vogue*'s 21 Under 21 list.

A TRUE STARR

Amandla Stenberg shot to superstardom after playing Rue in *The Hunger Games* and Starr in *The Hate U Give*. In their role as Starr, Amandla played an accidental activist. But they're an activist in real life too—and not accidentally.

At age 16, Amandla opened up to fans on Tumblr about being **nonbinary**—not identifying as either male or female.

"Being beautiful means confidently knowing that you're enough just the way you are." —Kheris Rogers
FEATUREFLASH PHOTO AGENCY/ SHUTTERSTOCK.COM

The name Amandla comes from the Zulu and Xhosa word for power.
GAGE SKIDMORE/WIKIMEDIA COMMONS/ CC BY-SA 3.0

They wrote about the importance of having the freedom to find one's own identity. Now in their 20s, Amandla continues to advocate for open conversation and less hate. As they said in an Insta caption, "Discussions are healthy. Ignorance is not."

Amandla is one of many LGBTQ2+ youth using the internet to take action on a variety of issues. Many sign petitions and join campaigns. Others write their own content and narratives. And there are plenty of topics to tackle. Compared to other youth, LGBTQ+ youth are far more likely to develop mental illnesses, become homeless or experience bullying and isolation.

We might think of young people as more accepting, but in the United States, the number of 18- to 34-year-olds who identify as **allies** to LGBTQ2+ people has been slowly and steadily dropping since 2016. Dropping! By speaking out, celebrities like Amandla create a path for others to follow.

SOCIAL MEDIA SMARTS

It's not hard to take action in support of the LGBT2Q+ community. Here are some ways you can be an ally:

- **Put your pronouns in your social media bios.** Do you go by *she/her* or *he/him* or *they/them* or something else? Trans people are often targeted for having their pronouns on their accounts. Cisgender people can help combat that sort of discrimination by putting pronouns in their own bios and normalizing the practice.

- **Recognize your privilege and use it for good.** Correct people who misgender others online, and speak up when you see someone using hate speech or slurs.

- **Educate yourself.** It isn't the responsibility of LGBT2Q+ people to teach the masses. Cis people should do their own research.

- **Realize you're not perfect.** If you misstep and get corrected, take it with humility and respect. Say, "I obviously have a lot to learn. I'll do better next time."

UNEXPECTED WINDOWS

Bana Alabed could hear a plane overhead, growing louder and louder.

Time to go home, her teacher said. It was too dangerous to stay at school.

But seven-year-old Bana was only partway to her house when she heard a huge explosion behind her. A bomb destroyed her school.

Bana was caught in the middle of the 2016 siege of Aleppo, Syria. Because anti-government groups had control of the city, the government cut all supply lines. Store shelves were bare. Overhead, Russian warplanes supported the government with repeated air strikes.

To a seven-year-old, this meant days of eating only rice and macaroni. It meant constant fear. Lack of sleep. And it meant losing her friend Yasmin, who was killed by yet another bombing.

"Does anyone know what has happened to us?" Bana asked her mom.

Between 2011 and 2021, more than 5.5 million Syrians fled to neighboring countries. Another 6.5 million lost or left their homes and sought safety in other parts of the country.

QASIOUN NEWS AGENCY - YOUTUBE/ WIKIMEDIA COMMONS/CC BY 3.0

Inspired by her daughter's words, Bana's mom opened a Twitter account so Bana could tell her own story to the world.

My name is Bana, I'm 7 years old. I am talking to the world now live from East #Aleppo. This is my last moment to either live or die.

She continued documenting her experiences for months, giving outsiders an intimate and frightening look at what her life was like. Soon she had hundreds of thousands of followers.

In December, six months after the siege began, Bana's family found temporary safety in Turkey. And a year later Bana published a book about her experiences.

Did Bana's online actions stop a war or save lives? No. But they helped thousands of people around the world understand what was happening in Syria...all through the eyes of a girl.

EMBRACING THE OCTOPUS

We like to hang out with people who are similar to us. In scientific terms, that's called an *affinity bias.* But if we befriend only people like ourselves, we never learn or experience anything new. We don't get to see the world from other perspectives.

There's another idea called *the contact hypothesis.* It's a big name for a simple idea. If you hang out with people who are different than you, you'll discover you have things in common. You'll carry fewer stereotypes and become more open-minded.

On social media, it's so easy to connect with people from different backgrounds and ethnicities. Maybe a new friendship is a click and a like away. And maybe, if enough of us make contact, entire systems will start to change.

American psychologist Gordon Allport came up with the contact hypothesis way back in 1954.

INSTA_PHOTOS/SHUTTERSTOCK.COM

The way we react to things is often influenced by our level of privilege. If you're a popular, straight-A student, you might find it easier to speak up against bullying than someone who's shy and new to the school. So use your privilege for good!

SOLSTOCK/GETTY IMAGES

SOCIAL MEDIA SMARTS

When you see discrimination online, you have a few options:

- **Report it**. Social media platforms have rules of conduct. The more people that report an offensive user, the more likely the platform will take action.

- **Ignore it**. Sometimes this is the best way to stay safe. You don't have to take responsibility for fixing the whole world.

- **Block the offensive user**. It doesn't have to be your job to educate other people. It can be exhausting!

- **Try the educational route**. If you see people silencing Black voices by saying, "All lives matter," you might create your own post explaining that Black people are killed more often by police.

- **Say what you think**. "Hey, that was hurtful. I'm offended, and I wish you wouldn't post things like that."

Remember that online abuse is *not okay*! So be respectful of others, even when they're annoying. And if someone targets you personally, be sure to report it to the social media platform, a parent or teacher, and—if necessary—the police.

HOW TO MAKE THE BES

MOM
Dinner's ready

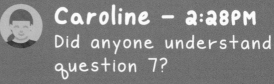

#homeworkclub

Caroline – 2:28PM
Did anyone understand question 7?

Tina – 2:30PM
That one stumped me too!

Penelope – 2:30PM
I got it! I think we were supposed to carry over the....

Four
TEACHING WITH TECH
Learning and Sharing Online

As COVID-19 swept the world in 2020 and 2021, schools from Austria to Australia switched abruptly to online learning. Teachers recorded lessons on Zoom or Microsoft Teams. Group projects shifted from coil-bound notebooks to Google Docs. Study groups became Discord chats.

In some cases, students flourished. They loved working from a corner of the kitchen, without the distractions of a busy classroom. Others quickly tired of hearing their teachers say, "Please mute your microphones" and "Stop posting memes in the chat bar, immediately."

Both the good and the bad of emergency learning prompted researchers to take a second look at online schooling. What role was the internet playing in kids' education? And what uses could social media have in the future of learning?

From people developing programs for girls in remote regions of Africa to teen TV stars advocating self-love,

Online learning feels entirely different if you have limited space and siblings arguing behind you.
FIZKES/SHUTTERSTOCK.COM

55

innovators were already using social media in creative ways. Post-pandemic, there are all sorts of new frontiers to explore.

PICKING POWER

Let's have a vote. Who wants to learn long division?

Nouns and verbs? Anyone? Anyone?

This is *not* the way we choose our school curricula. What we learn in school varies in different parts of the world and depends on all sorts of factors:

- Culture. Do people in your country value math skills more highly than music?
- History. What major events have changed the way people in your area think, act or work?
- Economy. What workers are needed, and what training do those workers need?

You might notice what's not on this list. *Your* preferences! Politicians, teachers and parents make the choices. Unless you're homeschooled by particularly flexible types, you're learning what the textbooks tell you.

If you were in charge of your school curriculum, how would you change things? What subjects would you add and which would you cross off the list?

BEARFOTOS/SHUTTERSTOCK.COM

#NoFilter

Tanya: When we were in quarantine during the COVID-19 pandemic, you studied cupcake-baking, pasta-making and French.

Julia: At least my choices were practical. You took an online poetry course.

Tanya: I admit, your hobbies were more useful. You make perfect ravioli.

Julia: Thanks to YouTube. Which proves it's possible to learn new skills on social media.

Tanya: Is there professional ravioli-making in your future?

Julia: You never know…

Tanya: And maybe my next book will be way more poetic!

Julia: We could write it together.

Tanya: *Poems about Pasta!*

Julia: Or not.

But after school, it's a whole different world—a world that includes video games, internet searches and social media.

Research in the United States suggests that when university students spend hours on Facebook and Twitter, their grades suffer. That makes sense. Too much multitasking and too little studying! But what about when students use the internet for research or scan social media for articles and links?

In one Dutch study, researchers worked with hundreds of high school teachers to track the possible connections between social media and schoolwork. About half the teachers provided YouTube videos or other social media links to help students explore topics further on their own time. (In teacher terms, this is called encouraging *self-regulated learning*.) But hardly any teachers used social media inside the classroom.

Julia's Headspace

In my 11th-grade social studies class, we were asked to create a community initiative. Two friends and I decided we wanted to educate students about feminism, something we'd never learned about when we were younger. We created lesson plans, an Instagram page and a website, then began teaching online workshops at schools across the city. And we're still going! Our organization is called The Daily Feminist. It's one of the most meaningful things I've ever been part of, and I'm so glad I did it!

If you have an idea, don't wait until after university. Spend some time searching online for grants in your city or region. Look for the support of an adult, like a teacher or parent, to help get you off the ground!

Minecraft fans say the game promotes creativity and problem-solving.
BLOOMICON/SHUTTERSTOCK.COM

A smaller study in Portugal found the same thing—teens rarely used the internet during class. But after school, they opened YouTube to learn video-game strategies and cell-phone fixes. They searched for homework help on forums and shared test-preparation notes on Messenger.

One student said video games had sparked his interest in ancient Japan and World War II history. A 12-year-old found her schoolwork on rocks easier because she'd learned about minerals while playing *Minecraft*. Still other students reported that by using social media and the internet after school, they developed more curiosity, surprised themselves with new skills and interests, and learned to try new strategies when the first ones didn't succeed.

After hearing these comments, the Portuguese researchers decided there was a growing gap in the lives of young people. On one side of the gap was traditional school, with subjects chosen by adults. On the other side was the freedom of digital learning. The students easily recognized that gap. But did the schools? Not so much.

Would you say the same about your school? In many places, it seems like traditional education needs to start building virtual bridges.

TAKING THE STAGE

Access to education isn't equal. In many parts of the world, girls face major barriers. Some of them can't afford school uniforms. Some stay home to care for family members. Others are forced into early marriages.

In Ethiopia, only 52 percent of girls attend school. The average marriage age in some regions is 15, and many girls are mothers by the time they're 18.

Could a combination of social media and pop music change things for the better? That's what a nonprofit organization called Girl Effect wanted to know. It funded not a school, not a series of workshops, but...

...a girl band!

Girl Effect recruited five Ethiopian pop musicians, with the stage names Lemlem, Emuye, Sara, Mimi and Melat, to form the band Yegna. The group's first concert was free as long as attendees met two qualifications—be a girl and bring a girl.

In 2013 and 2014, Yegna released songs about girl power and ending violence against women. They were wildly popular. Soon the musicians were sharing their girl-empowerment messages with more than eight million fans via Facebook, a YouTube channel and a weekly radio drama. They also used these platforms to amplify the voices of girls from rural areas and from disadvantaged families.

According to UNICEF, a third of the girls in the world's poorest households are unlikely to attend primary school.
PER-ANDERS PETTERSSON/GETTY IMAGES

There was just one problem. The project was partly funded by the British government's foreign-aid department. And when the British press found out money was going to a girl band, outrage erupted. That money could be better spent on British seniors in need! *The Daily Mail* called Yegna the most "wasteful, ludicrous and patronizing" aid project in Africa.

Some politicians leaped to the band's defense, saying aid was about more than delivering food packages. According to Girl Effect's research, three-quarters of girl listeners said Yegna had helped inspire them to continue their education. And most male listeners said the band helped change views about forced marriages. But public opinion had turned against Yegna—at least in Britain. Funding for the project was cut in 2017.

That didn't stop the organizers at the center of the project. There are now five new performers involved in Yegna, and they've launched a TV series. In its first season, the show reached more than nine million viewers. Meanwhile, the original performers have continued their girl-power hits under a new band name, Endegna.

Do you think you absorb values and ideas from pop music? Could it be an important way to reach young people?

GIRL EFFECT

GETTING EXPERIMENTAL

Peru's Mini Academy of Science and Technology was about to begin. Organizers were sure 2020 would be the best session yet.

The Mini Academy selects 40 girls each year to attend workshops, where they complete hands-on experiments and work with real scientists. Science education in Peru has significant gaps, especially for girls, and the Mini Academy had already won a major UNESCO prize for its work.

But...disaster! Just a week before the 2020 program was supposed to begin, COVID-19 forced Peru to close its schools!

Mini Academy president Johanna Johnson scrambled to adapt. She had dozens of 8- to 11-year-old girls depending on her. Could they switch to online learning? Well, there were problems with computer access to sort out first. Even in Lima, the capital city of Peru, only 60 percent of families have an internet connection.

Then, once she had managed to digitally connect with the students, Johanna had to find ways to maintain the Mini Academy's focus on hands-on learning. She and her instructors found experiments girls could do with basic household materials. Since the students had countless questions about COVID-19, they incorporated pandemic research.

Nine-year-old Samantha was one of the 2020 students. "I really like learning more about the coronavirus," she said. "My mother always says it is important not to believe everything we hear and to always investigate and find out the truth."

Using simple supplies, participants built model viruses as they discussed the impacts of the COVID-19 pandemic.
MINI ACADEMIA DE CIENCIA Y TECNOLOGÍA (MACTEC)

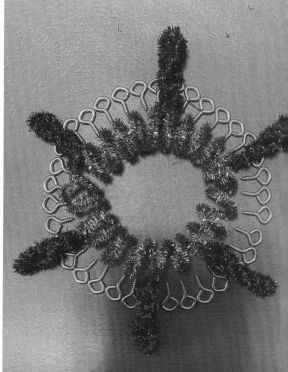

Do you like to finish your homework right away, or are you more like feminist writer Rita Mae Brown? She once said, "If it weren't for the last minute, nothing would get done."

ALYS TOMLINSON/GETTY IMAGES

SOCIAL MEDIA SMARTS

You signed up for an online origami class. You were super excited, and your first folded frog turned out great. You were planning to do the second class. Well, you're still planning to do the second class. You just haven't had time yet. And okay, that folded frog has been sitting on your desk for a year…

This happens to all of us. We get excited, and then we get distracted. But there are a few ways we can boost our follow-through abilities, if we really want to learn:

- **Set a schedule**. Decide what day of the week and what time of day you're going to do your online learning. Then write it in your calendar and set an alarm on your computer.

- **Clear some space**. Your origami will seem more motivating if you're not trying to do it in the middle of your laundry pile. Make like a professional and set aside a work area.

- **Enlist a coach**. We all do better when someone checks on us. Ask a friend to remind and encourage you. Better yet, sign up together!

FROM SEX ED TO SEXTING

From Cairo to Calgary and Beijing to Boston, girls are turning to social media for one specific kind of curriculum. Sex ed.

In the United States, the spectrum of health education offered in school has steadily narrowed. While parents and politicians argue over what should be taught, school districts quietly remove topics from the curriculum. The Guttmacher Institute in New York found that between 2006 and 2013 there were significant drops in what girls learned in school about birth control, sexually transmitted diseases and HIV/AIDS. Declines were worse for girls than for boys, and they were particularly bad in rural areas.

The United States isn't alone. Some countries offer no formal sex education. So in the absence of formal lessons, where do girls turn to? Social media, of course. It's much easier to anonymously type a question than raise a hand in class!

A study at Duke University in North Carolina found that both teens *and* their doctors were reluctant to talk about sex during office visits.

SDI PRODUCTIONS/GETTY IMAGES

There is plenty of terrible advice on the internet. No, random Twitter user, it's *not* necessary to shower twice a day when you have your period. And disinfectant wipes don't cure rashes.

Fortunately there are also sites with actual, reliable health information. *Go Ask Alice!* was founded by Columbia University's health-promotion program in 1993. A year later the site was made publicly available on the internet. The doctors and med students behind the project now answer thousands of questions for millions of users each year, about everything from bulimia to breast-reduction surgery.

Meanwhile, governments and other official health-care organizations have noticed girls' pivot toward internet health info. And they're working to reach those girls in new ways. One team, led by Lynae Brayboy at Brown University, developed an app called Girl Talk to provide sex-ed information to teens. They gave the app to a test group for two weeks and noticed significant changes in the girls' understanding

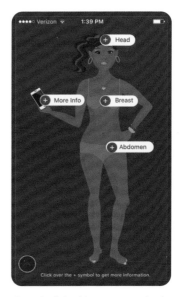

The Girl Talk health app was used only for a study, but it provided data that researchers hope will help in designing similar apps in the future.

GIRL TALK

Julia's Headspace

To me, social media seems to offer all sorts of new opportunities. How can we harness the power of the internet to continue closing gender gaps? How can we share our passions? What do we want to learn (and teach) online? And how quickly can we figure it out and launch our projects, the way some of the girls in this book did?

We still need more research about how to reach girls with health information and how doctors can best answer their questions online.

BISERKA STOJANOVIC/GETTY IMAGES

of anatomy, sexuality and relationships, and sexually transmitted disease prevention. So five stars to Girl Talk!

But it's not all about sex. In British Columbia, the government used social media to reach young people during the COVID-19 pandemic. The premier reached out on Twitter to stars such as Ryan Reynolds and Seth Rogan, asking them to help spread safety messages. (Both responded, with Ryan Reynolds famously telling people, "Don't kill my mom.") Then the government released a series of TikTok videos featuring a young health official who happened to be a stand-up comedian on the side. (What to say when someone offers a sip of their drink? "Hell no.")

It's difficult to know whether these interventions made a difference in the number of COVID-19 infections. But the campaign showed that even governments are paying attention to the connections between young people, health and social media.

MIND-BODY BATTLES

This book highlights the good things about social media. But there's a dark side too. **Cyberbullying**, unachievable standards and edited photos reign across the internet. It can be difficult not to absorb the anxiety and negativity.

Researchers in Britain are tracking 19,000 young people as part of something called the Millennium Cohort Study. They've found that twice as many girls as boys are on social media for more than three hours a day. And the more hours a girl spends online, the more likely she is to experience symptoms of depression. The researchers can't be certain whether time online causes depression or whether unhappy people are more likely to turn to social media. But they *think* it's probably the former.

So how can girls stay positive and appreciate themselves when the internet's bringing them down? Fortunately there are more and more people online advocating for improving mental health and practicing self-love! Millie Bobby Brown, who began playing Eleven on *Stranger Things* when she was only 12, has been open about her life as a child star and the mental-health strains involved. On her 16th birthday, she talked about the effects media has had on her as a teenage girl. She posted a montage of headlines on Instagram.

"*Stranger Things* star leaves Twitter after cyberbullying."

"Millie Bobby Brown criticized for adult style."

By opening up about cyberbullying, celebrities like Millie Bobby Brown make it easier for regular girls to recognize and deal with haters on social media.
FEATUREFLASH/DREAMSTIME.COM

She wrote that she was "frustrated from the inaccuracy, inappropriate comments, sexualization and unnecessary insults that ultimately have resulted in pain and insecurity." Despite the bullying, however, Millie continues to speak her mind and pursue her passions.

"Not ever will I be defeated. I'll continue doing what I love and spreading the message in order to make change."

SHARING IS CARING, RIGHT?

There are tons of websites and apps teaching things to girls. Then there's another category of platforms meant to empower girls to learn. And there's a third set of initiatives—places where girls reach out to other girls to share and exchange knowledge.

Today's girls face challenges no previous generation has faced. Given global warming, systemic racism and divisive politics, it can seem as if the apocalypse is right around the corner. Meanwhile, there's a pile of math homework and a never-ending text stream to manage. Who better to help girls juggle all of this than other girls?

As more and more young people learn to code, and as they launch their own blogs, podcasts, apps and platforms, we might see a whole new era of education.

#NoFilter

Julia: Social media can be exhausting, and it's bound to take a toll. It's important to take care of yourself and your mental health and find good coping mechanisms that work for you!

Tanya: Agreed. And it's also important—for all of us, not just kids and teens—to put our phones away at night and get some sleep.

Julia: Wow. Thank you for the enlightening public health message, Mom.

Tanya: You're *so* welcome. Now hand it over.

If you could choose anything to learn online, what would it be? (There's probably a virtual course available!)
PHYNART STUDIO/GETTY IMAGES

Kids are using various teaching platforms to launch their own classes and workshops. Julia Kyi taught her first online course when she was in eighth grade. It was called Academy for Action, and it was funded by a small grant from the City of Vancouver.

LAURA OLIVAS/GETTY IMAGES

SOCIAL MEDIA SMARTS

Ever consider launching your own online class? Maybe your idea is an educational TikTok series, a YouTube course or a Zoom workshop. Maybe you're an expert in coding languages or a whiz at cake icing. Whatever your talent and whatever your platform, here are a few things to keep in mind:

- **Start small.** Post your info on your social media channels. Share with friends and family. Ask your mom to spread the word. Don't worry if you only get three sign-ups. If people enjoy your work, they'll tell their friends!

- **Plan, plan and plan.** The better your preparations, the more smoothly your lessons will go. Include a mix of facts, real-life stories and exercises for your students to try. Keep a couple of additional ideas on hand, in case you have extra time.

- **Banish the butterflies.** *No one* delivers perfect online workshops. Keep it casual, and be willing to laugh at your own mistakes. If you get overwhelmed, ask some questions. Even if you're on YouTube or TikTok, you can pause, breathe and give your viewers a moment to consider.

- **Celebrate your achievements!** Teaching isn't easy, especially online. Celebrate the things that went well, make a few notes about things to change next time, and start planning workshop two!

Five
VIRAL VOICES
Taking the Lead Online

You can't vote. You can't run for office. You probably can't donate millions to your favorite cause. So how are you supposed to influence the world?

For some people, the answer lies in the power of social media.

Over the past decade, girls have become outspoken advocates for change. They've used Instagram posts to spark global climate marches, Twitter and Facebook posts to argue for gun control, and online petitions to help ban plastic bags.

In 2018 a speech to the United Nations General Assembly by a 13-year-old Indigenous activist named Autumn Peltier went viral. She asked world leaders to protect waterways by giving them the same rights as humans. And Autumn had a call for both politicians and ordinary citizens: "Now is the time to warrior up and take a stand for our planet."

Young people around the world are following her lead.

To be an activist, you don't need a great hand-painted sign. (But it doesn't hurt to have one!)

X González is now pursuing a college degree in activism. They continue to speak out about gun violence.
LEV RADIN/SHUTTERSTOCK.COM

Gun violence is 25 times higher in the United States than it is in other high-income countries. Someone is shot and killed once every 15 minutes.
JUSTIN STARR PHOTOGRAPHY/
SHUTTERSTOCK.COM

DODGING BULLETS

On Valentine's Day in 2018, X González was in the auditorium of Marjory Stoneman Douglas High in Parkland, Florida. When the fire alarm sounded, they filed out to the hallway. But X and their fellow students were told to turn around and shelter in place. For the next two hours, X huddled at the back of the auditorium, searching their phone for updates on an active shooter.

Meanwhile, a 19-year-old former student was roaming the school with a semiautomatic rifle.

The Parkland shooting was just one in a series of American massacres. The United States has less than 5 percent of the world's population, but almost half of the world's guns. And the country has had more than twice as many school shootings as the rest of the world combined.

The Parkland event was particularly deadly—the shooter killed 17 people that day. At a candlelight vigil after the shooting, X gave an interview to CNN. On February 17, they gave a speech at a gun-control rally in Fort Lauderdale. They wiped away tears as they spoke, but their words were clear, angry and pointed.

If the president wants to come up to me and tell me to my face that it was a terrible tragedy and how it should never have happened and maintain telling us how nothing is going to be done about it, I'm going to happily ask him how much money he received from the National Rifle Association. You want to know something? It doesn't matter, because I already know. Thirty million dollars.

The video of their speech drew thousands of likes, shares and comments. Soon X teamed up with fellow students, including Cameron Kasky, David Hogg and Jaclyn Corin, to create the #NeverAgain movement. They announced a list of

The March for Our Lives in 2018 drew students, teachers, parents and supporters to Washington, DC.

demands, including stricter gun-control regulations. They planned a march. And when they weren't fielding media requests, X and their fellow campaigners spent their time quashing pro-gun arguments on social media. Jen Golbeck, an associate professor at the University of Maryland's College of Information Studies, called the Parkland students "a wonderful counterpoint to...this machine of right-wing propaganda."

Within days of the shooting, X's new Twitter account had 300,000 followers—far outnumbering those of the National Rifle Association (NRA), the organization lobbying hard against gun-control laws. Cameron's Facebook page gained another 35,000 supporters. Their social media presence helped the teens keep the Parkland story in the news and keep pressure on politicians. They also raised four million dollars via the crowd-funding platform GoFundMe and inspired millions more in donations from celebrities such as Oprah Winfrey. On March 24, 2018, the movement's March for Our Lives drew hundreds of thousands of gun-control advocates to Washington and to more than 800 partner events across the country.

In March 2018, Florida passed the Marjory Stoneman Douglas High School Public Safety Act, increasing the legal age for firearms ownership, requiring background checks and barring potentially violent people from owning guns. It was the first time the state had passed new gun-control regulations in 30 years.

Many real-life marches and protests now include simultaneous social media actions. People who can't attend can help boost a movement's reach by reposting photos and encouraging others to join.

MIKE PAROLINI/SHUTTERSTOCK.COM

THE DARK SIDE OF SURVIVAL

When the Parkland survivors took a stand on social media for gun control, many people disagreed with them. Pro-gun Americans were quick to send insults—and even death threats. Conspiracy theorists claimed the Parkland teens were "crisis actors" pretending to have been students in the school where the shooting occurred. Following X González's speech at the March for Our Lives, pro-gun advocates photoshopped a *Teen Vogue* video of the activist to make it look as if they had ripped up a copy of the US Constitution. X faced backlash as the fake video spread across online platforms.

The survivors responded with yearbooks, photos and other proof they were real Parkland students, not actors. Platforms such as Twitter promised to take steps to control the harassment. But eventually at least one of the students had to suspend his Facebook account.

These student activists weren't the first to face cyberbullying, and they won't be the last. Online it's particularly easy for people to start heated debates, harass people and hurl abuse. Unfortunately, most trolls face minimal

Even when mean comments are posted by people who live far away, they can make us feel hurt, angry and unsafe. Take a screenshot, then tell a trusted adult.

MONKEY BUSINESS IMAGES/
SHUTTERSTOCK.COM

consequences. And even students posting the most innocent content—whether it's knitting on Etsy or dancing on TikTok—can find themselves facing haters. In the United States, about 15 percent of students report experiencing cyberbullying, and studies have linked online harassment to anxiety, depression and even suicide.

Nadia S. Ansary is a professor at Rider University in New Jersey. She's spent years examining cyberbullying and the programs in place to prevent it. Many of these programs are add-ons to traditional anti-bullying campaigns. And Nadia believes that's a mistake. To combat online harassment, she thinks we need more

- specific, school-wide programs
- educated and involved parents
- friends and bystanders willing to report harassment
- social media companies that better protect their users
- counselors who recognize the risks
- laws to target online abusers

While some of these changes are underway, there's still a world of hate out there. And yet teens keep fighting. They keep creating. Many remain committed to overcoming the harassment and spreading their truths.

We need to protect ourselves and each other from cyberbullying. All members of our community, even our best friends, play a role.
KLAUS VEDFELT/GETTY IMAGES

SOCIAL MEDIA SMARTS

A study by the non-profit organization Plan International found that almost 60 percent of girls and women encountered verbal abuse online. And the Cyberbullying Research Center in the United States says about 15 percent of tweens are targets. Yikes!

We shouldn't have to accept hate as an everyday part of the internet. If you're getting cyberbullied, you have options. Here's some advice from the RCMP, Canada's police force.

- Leave the online conversation.

- Keep track of the bullying with screenshots.

- Tell a trusted adult what's happening.

- **Report the abuse.** Submit a complaint to your social media platform. If you're getting abuse from someone at school, talk to your principal. If someone's threatening you, call the police.

Some activists love the spotlight, but others are introverts who care so much about an issue, they're driven to speak up.

DIEGO G DIAZ/SHUTTERSTOCK.COM

THE ACTIVE INGREDIENTS

½ cup idealism

½ cup frustration

1 cup hope

What exactly *is* the recipe for an activist?

Jessica Taft is a professor at the University of California at Santa Cruz. She interviewed 75 girl activists from across North and South America. Jessica asked each girl to describe how her convictions began.

In some ways, their stories were dramatically different. A few experienced sudden aha moments and knew they needed to speak out about an issue. Others felt a growing awareness of the world's problems. Some had less involved parents, and others grew up in activist homes. (When a Mexican middle-school student named Ramona rebelled against her school's strict dress code, her parents were called.

But when they arrived at the school, they started handing out flyers in Ramona's defense!)

Despite their differences, many of the girls shared common emotions and experiences. Here are a few of the similarities Jessica found in her research:

- Many girls felt separated from other teens. Their interests were different and their convictions stronger.
- Through friends, family members or by chance, many found activist communities to join.
- The girls didn't feel as if they were rebelling against their parents, but their convictions and their methods were often different from those of previous generations. Sometimes even supportive parents didn't fully understand climate change, for example, or know how to use social media.

As she completed her interviews, Jessica noticed one other thing. The girls didn't emphasize their own heroics or the ways they'd overcome barriers. They weren't necessarily "activists," some of the girls told her. They were still "becoming." They thought of themselves as learning and growing, looking for more ways to make the world better for everyone.

#NoFilter

Tanya: I really want to share your "save the whales" letter from elementary school.

Julia: Absolutely not.

Tanya: Part of the letter?

Julia: No! I was eight! It's embarrassing.

Tanya: One sentence?

Julia: Argh. Fine.

Tanya: Here it is: "Whale hunting is cruel, mean, and unfair, and every whale in the world agrees with me."

Julia: Well…I stand by the basic idea. They would if they could!

Julia's Headspace

Solidarity! Guess who inspired Greta with the idea of a school strike? The teen gun-control activists of Parkland, FL. When you're organizing online, you have no idea how far your message might travel or who it might affect. Don't be scared to reach out to other activists and ask for retweets, links and support. You might find allies in unexpected places!

"Some people say that I should study to become a climate scientist so that I can 'solve the climate crisis.' But the climate crisis has already been solved. We already have all the facts and solutions. All we have to do is to wake up and change." —Greta Thunberg
1000 WORDS/SHUTTERSTOCK.COM

STRIKE ZONE

In August 2018, Greta Thunberg settled herself outside the Swedish parliament with a hand-written sign reading *skolstrejk för klimatet*, or "school strike for climate." She was 15 years old and entirely alone on the cobblestones. But after Greta posted her image on Instagram and Twitter, it didn't take long to gain attention.

Local reporters soon showed up. A major bank representative with a huge Twitter following retweeted her photo. On the second day of her strike, she was joined by a teen trans and environmental activist named Mayson Persson. On the third day about 35 people showed up. And a year later there were more.

Millions more.

Greta has a form of autism spectrum disorder (ASD). Once she learned about the effects of climate change, she couldn't ignore them. She felt compelled to act and to motivate others to act. On September 20, 2019, just over a year after her protest began, Greta addressed the thousands of protesters who had gathered for the Global Climate Strike in New York City. In towns and cities around the world, four million people demonstrated that day. They were part of a new school-strike movement called Fridays for Future.

Remember Julie Zeilinger's *FBomb* blog from chapter 1? It's now part of the Women's Media Center, which was cofounded by Jane Fonda in 2005.
PHIL PASQUINI/SHUTTERSTOCK.COM

Young people weren't the only ones inspired by Greta's call. Jane Fonda has been speaking her mind to politicians and world leaders since the 1960s, when she supported the civil rights movement and vocally opposed the Vietnam War. When she learned of Greta's campaign, Jane partnered with Greenpeace and other environmental groups to launch Fire Drill Fridays. Each weekly event focuses on a different aspect of the climate emergency, and each showcases a new array of speakers—often celebrities.

The activists responding to Greta's call are angry and frustrated, and they're taking action. Greta has translated her lone school strike and a few social media images to a global movement of millions. And today she keeps her followers updated and motivated with posts on Instagram and Twitter. She also uses her platforms to highlight the work of other young climate activists from around the world.

Melati and Isabel Wijsen attended Green School Bali, a school dedicated to sustainability.

JENYA KADNIKOVA

GOING GLOBAL

Sisters Melati and Isabel Wijsen grew up on the island of Bali in Indonesia. In 2013, when they were 10 and 12 years old, they listened one day as their teacher described significant world leaders—Nelson Mandela, who fought against apartheid in South Africa, Lady Diana, who campaigned against land mines and raised money for more than 100 charities, and Mahatma Gandhi, who led India's campaign for independence.

As the sisters walked home that afternoon, they decided they wanted to be significant too. So they plopped themselves on their sofa and began brainstorming. What were Bali's problems? Which ones could they solve?

Bali's economy relies on tourism. And one of the island's biggest problems was easy to spot, scattered on the beaches—plastic. The island created enough garbage to fill a 14-story building every day. Less than 5 percent of plastic bags were recycled.

By the end of the girls' brainstorming session, Bye Bye Plastic Bags had been born. After gathering a group of friends and supporters, Melati and Isabel launched a global online petition, as well as a real-life version. They created educational presentations for other kids, they set up information booths at markets and festivals, and they began distributing reusable bags.

After years of campaigning, they finally received an invitation to meet with Bali's governor. And later that day, as a result of their meeting, the governor signed a promise to help Bali go plastic-free. Since then Bye Bye Plastic Bags has used social media to promote local plastic-free businesses. Melati and Isabel recorded a TED talk and spoke to United Nations delegates. And in 2018 the island of Bali officially banned single-use plastic bags.

Melati and Isabel weren't born to power. They didn't have tons of money, media connections or political influence. What they did have was conviction, dedication and the power of social media. The internet allows activists to reach beyond their local communities and build global support. A retweet from a celebrity can bring instant attention. A retweet from a politician can prompt media coverage, discussion and even legislative change.

Plastic isn't only an Indonesian problem. People around the world dump an estimated nine million tons (eight million metric tons) into the ocean each year.

KOLDUNOV/GETTY IMAGES

The Wijsen sisters recently launched a new organization called Youthtopia, aimed at helping inspire and train a new generation of activists.

MARIA SYMCHYCH-NAVROTSKA/ GETTY IMAGES

Julia's Headspace

Do you have a passion, a project or an opinion? Because the next global movement is only a few clicks away, and you might be the one to lead it.

At one time activists were limited to learning from those in their own cities or neighborhoods. Today they have global support at their fingertips.

PROSTOCK-STUDIO/SHUTTERSTOCK.COM

Miriam Sobré-Denton is an assistant professor at Texas State University. She studies the ways that social media helps grassroots movements reach global scale. We all know the internet can help reach more people. But Miriam points out other ways social media can grow a campaign:

- It lets activists share resources. A small group in one country might highlight a movement in another, and vice versa.
- It helps minority groups, which might be separated by geography, culture or religion, to reach past real-life barriers. On social media, people are more equal than they are in real life.
- It allows activists to learn from others. What worked for previous campaigns? What are other protesters planning?

Together, activists can gain attention, support and funding—even when their real lives exist on separate continents. Social media helped Melati and Isabel enlist the support of some of the thousands of tourists and celebrities who visit Bali. Eventually it helped them change their world.

"Our country's government is still granting our territories to the corporations responsible of climate change. This is criminal."
Those were Helena Gualinga's words at the 2019 UN Climate Change Conference in Madrid, Spain.

SPEAKING TRUTH TO POWER

Helena Gualinga, an Indigenous teen from the Amazon, is speaking her truth to the Ecuadorian government. Her traditional lands in the rainforest are sought after by oil companies and by the Ecuadorian military. In her speeches to the government and the United Nations, Helena champions climate action and Indigenous rights, and fights for her home to remain protected. Through posts, stories and comments, she also builds online communities to support her cause. (She has almost 80,000 Instagram followers.)

Helena shares the campaigns of other young activists, explains issues of pollution and worker exploitation, and calls out global leaders, all in Insta captions. One of her posts reads:

INDIGENOUS BLOOD, NOT A SINGLE DROP MORE!
As we are facing one of the biggest crisis in human history, climate change. Indigenous people, protectors of the amazon and preventers of further climate destruction are criminalized, persecuted and murdered for defending LIFE and BASIC HUMAN RIGHTS. STAND WITH INDIGENOUS PEOPLE!

With words like these, she is an advocate for her people and the rights of Indigenous people worldwide.

Mari Copeny's activism brought former president Barack Obama to Flint, MI, where the pair met backstage at Northwestern High School.

FLICKR.COM/OBAMA WHITE HOUSE ARCHIVED/OFFICIAL WHITE HOUSE PHOTO BY PETE SOUZA

There is always power in numbers. The more voices you can raise, the better!

NICKYLLOYD/GETTY IMAGES

In Michigan, another young girl is fighting for her own community. Mari Copeny, better known as Little Miss Flint, has been advocating for safe drinking water since she was eight years old. The water in her hometown of Flint, Michigan, is contaminated with lead, which can cause health problems and even death. In 2016 Mari wrote a letter to then president Obama, discussing the problem and asking to meet with him. The president replied and came to visit Mari in Flint.

It was a grand gesture, but the water quality didn't change. So meeting the president became only the beginning of Mari's activism. She took to Twitter, using the platform to advocate and fundraise. In 2019 she started #WednesdaysForWater, highlighting a city without clean water every Wednesday. Today Mari is known worldwide, and she continues to use her social media to advocate change.

Mari and Helena are working on different issues, on different continents. But the two have a lot in common. When political leaders didn't help them, they became leaders. They both have big plans and ambitions, and they fight hard for their beliefs.

So how can the rest of us speak truth to power and make our voices heard?

ACTIVISM OR SLACKTIVISM?

Sign our petition with a single click.

> *Raise your voice for the cause! Please RT widely!*

"Like" our page and show your support.

We could spend all day clicking our way to a better world. Charities and activist groups say that online campaigns are the first step to raising awareness and growing public support. But is it true? Do our online actions lead to change? Or are they signs of **performative activism**?

The word slacktivism gained popularity in the late 1990s, to mock the way people were willing to support a cause...as long as it didn't cost real-life time or money.

Ask people to click? No problem.

Ask them to volunteer or donate? Crickets.

When someone signs a petition for your cause, you've gained a "passive ally." They're supportive, but they're not doing much. The next step is to reach your passive allies and inspire them to become active—to write letters, make calls or join marches.

#NoFilter

Tanya: I like that social media allows introverts to be activists. When I was on a school committee, trying to get the government to build an earthquake-safe elementary school, we used Twitter to rally parents, gather community support and directly contact politicians.

Julia: But you could have called them. Remember when I was 12 and starting my babysitting business, you offered me envelopes for my flyers?

Tanya: Because I assumed you would stuff the flyers in people's mailboxes and run. That's what I would have done. But you said you had to actually talk to potential clients.

Julia: Exactly.

Tanya: I'll stick to social media.

Julia: We've just discovered that it takes both extroverts and introverts to run a successful rebellion.

Tanya: May the odds be ever in our favor.

Katherine White is a professor at the University of British Columbia. She studies consumer behavior. She and her colleagues have done a series of studies on how and why people support causes. In one of those studies, a researcher offered poppies to students walking down a university hallway.

"Would you accept a free poppy to wear right now to show your support for veterans?" researchers asked.

At the other end of the hallway, a second researcher asked for donations. On average, the poppy-wearing students donated 34 cents to the cause.

Then the researchers changed one thing. Instead of giving students a visible poppy, they offered a poppy hidden inside an envelope. At the other end of the hallway, they again asked for donations. The students who accepted a poppy inside an envelope donated an average of 86 cents—more than twice as much!

Why would an envelope matter? Katherine's team suggested that students wearing poppies felt as if they'd already made a statement to the world. *Look at me! I support veterans! I'm a good person!*

Incidentally, poppies went viral long before the internet existed. John McCrae published the poem "In Flanders Fields" in 1915, during World War I. Wearing a poppy quickly became a symbol of remembrance of those who sacrificed their lives.
ELENATHEWISE/GETTY IMAGES

This sort of thing is called *impression management*. We want other people to think we're great. We like to project an ideal image, online and in real life. That means clicking on causes our friends support or Instagramming photos that will get us lots of likes. That kind of action, focused on other people, doesn't necessarily translate to bigger actions.

But the students who accepted a hidden poppy weren't thinking about the reactions of other people. They were more focused on their own morals. Accepting the hidden poppy reminded them to support veterans. When they reached the other end of the hall, a donation seemed a natural part of their own moral code. In the language of researchers, this is called *self-consistency*.

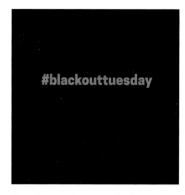

#blackouttuesday

Changing your Instagram feed or your Twitter photo for a day is one example of performative activism. If you want to take the next step, write an email or letter in support of the cause.

It's easier than ever before to contact politicians directly. And while you may be too young to vote, you're not too young to volunteer. If you have a strong opinion, join a phone bank or a canvassing team during election season.
1BSG/GETTY IMAGES

None of this answers the question of whether slacktivism is all good or all bad. So does Katherine think it's a good idea to support causes online? She says we should definitely add our support. Online movements can raise awareness and create momentum around a cause. But we also need to be aware that these simple actions might make us feel as if we've done our part. Saved the world with just one click. And that's simply not true.

If you really care, ask yourself what else you can do, online *and* in the real world.

TURNING UP THE VOLUME

Girls have always been amazing. And they've always had strong opinions.

Mabel Ping-Hua Lee emigrated from China to the United States when she was nine years old. In 1912, at age 16, she met with a group of suffragettes (women campaigning for the right to vote) in New York. They invited Mabel to help with their next demonstration. A few months later she rode with other organizers at the front of 10,000 marchers.

Later Mabel wrote this in *The Chinese Students' Monthly*: "Feminists want nothing more than the equality of opportunity for women to prove their merits and what they are best suited to do." She became the first Chinese woman in the United States to earn a PhD in economics and was a lifelong advocate for feminism and voting rights.

Inspiring 10,000 marchers in 1912 was an amazing feat, particularly for a person of color. But imagine what Mabel could have done with social media. Today she'd have millions of people following her lead. She could have exchanged tweets with politicians, distributed petitions to millions and shared her articles with her Facebook friends.

For the first time in history, girls have a public voice. Social media offers them the ability to build a platform just as visible and vocal as that of any politician. And with these new abilities, they're already changing the world.

Mabel Ping-Hau Lee began her activism in 1912. But because of laws that discriminated against Chinese immigrants, she didn't get the right to vote until 1943.

NATIONAL ARCHIVES/PUBLIC DOMAIN

SOCIAL MEDIA SMARTS

So you want to warrior up and become an activist? Here are some of the key steps taken by the campaigners in this chapter:

- **Find a cause (or causes) you care about**. From climate strikes to women's marches, there are many ways to make a difference.

- **Get involved**. Volunteer, go to events, and join online initiatives. Get out there and get active.

- **Build a community**. A group of young people can make a big difference, so gather as many friends and allies as you can, online and in real life. Support from powerful adults always helps too.

- **Speak your truth**. Write letters, start petitions, send emails and request meetings where you can speak directly to authority figures. Take action online and in real life.

- **Don't give up!** Activism isn't easy. You won't always be heard, and you might not see immediate results. Claim your space, know your power and keep fighting.

GLOSSARY

allies—in the world of social justice, an ally is a person of one social group who stands up in support of those from another group—usually a group facing discrimination

BIPOC—an abbreviation that stands for Black, Indigenous and People of Color

body positivity—a movement designed to empower people to love their own bodies

call-out—a type of public shaming in which people are targeted on social media for things they've written, said or created

cancel culture—withdrawing support for people or companies (particularly on social media) after they do something that's considered offensive or possibly criminal

cis—in reference to a person whose gender aligns with the sex they were assigned at birth

cupcake feminism—feminism designed for and by women of privilege, which fails to acknowledge the need for equity and intersectionality

cyberbullying—online harassment, via text messaging, social media or video game, that is intended to embarrass, threaten or silence someone

feminism—a movement that advocates for women to have the same opportunities and rights as men

fourth-wave feminism—the current wave of feminism, based largely online, that focuses on things such as sexual harassment, body positivity and the inclusion of underrepresented groups

Gen Z—people born between the mid-1990s and the early 2010s, the first generation to be raised with social media

hashtag feminism—a type of activism based mainly online, in which people use hashtags to collectively raise awareness of feminist issues

homophobia—irrational fear of and prejudice against LGBT2Q+ people

intersectional feminism—feminism inclusive of all marginalized groups

IRL—an abbreviation for *in real life*

LGBT2Q+—an abbreviation used for people of varying gender identities and sexualities: lesbian, gay, bisexual, transgender, Two-Spirit, queer and others

lynching—killing someone without a trial, usually by hanging; a type of mob violence once used against Black people in the United States

marginalized groups—communities that experience discrimination

microaggressions—commonplace actions or words that express prejudice

misogyny—hatred of or discrimination against women

nonbinary—not conforming to the binary classification of male or female

performative activism—supporting a cause to make oneself look good, rather than taking genuine action

privilege—social advantage gained without effort by virtue of class, wealth, race, sex or gender

sexism—discrimination based on gender, particularly discrimination against women

sexting—sending sexually explicit words or photos via text message

slacktivism—supporting a cause only when it's as easy and convenient as clicking a button online

stereotypes—generalized beliefs people have about other people, often based on their race, gender or sexuality

systemic bias—prejudices built into organization or government systems that create bias against minority groups

transphobia—irrational fear of and discrimination against transgender people

trolls—people who attack or harass other people online

RESOURCES

Books

Bartoletti, Susan Campbell. *How Women Won the Vote: Alice Paul, Lucy Burns, and Their Big Idea*. New York: Harper Collins, 2002.

Drake, Jane, and Ann Love. *Yes You Can! Your Guide to Becoming an Activist*. New York: Penguin Random House, 2010.

Falkowski, Melissa, and Eric Garner, eds. *We Say #NeverAgain: Reporting by the Parkland Student Journalists*. Toronto: Penguin Random House, 2018.

Humphreys, Jessica Dee, and Rona Ambrose. *The International Day of the Girl: Celebrating Girls Around the World*. Toronto: Kids Can Press, 2020.

In This Together Media, ed. *Nevertheless We Persisted: 48 Voices of Defiance, Strength, and Courage*. New York: Penguin Random House, 2019.

Kyi, Tanya Lloyd. *Eyes and Spies: How You're Tracked and Why You Should Know*. Toronto: Annick Press, 2017.

Kyi, Tanya Lloyd. *This Is Your Brain on Stereotypes: How Science Is Tackling Unconscious Bias*. Toronto: Kids Can Press, 2020.

Margolin, Jamie. *Youth to Power: Your Voice and How to Use It*. New York: Hachette Books, 2020.

Polak, Monique. *I Am a Feminist: Claiming the F-Word in Turbulent Times*. Victoria: Orca Book Publishers, 2019.

Stevenson, Robin. *My Body My Choice: The Fight for Abortion Rights*. Victoria: Orca Book Publishers, 2019.

Stevenson, Robin. *Pride: The Celebration and the Struggle*. Victoria: Orca Book Publishers, 2020.

Stone, Tanya Lee. *Girl Rising: Changing the World One Girl at a Time*. New York: Penguin Random House, 2017.

Styron, Alexandra. *Steal This Country: A Handbook for Resistance, Persistence, and Fixing Almost Everything*. New York: Penguin Random House, 2018.

Thunberg, Greta. *No One Is Too Small to Make a Difference*. New York: Penguin Random House, 2020.

Weiss, Elaine. *The Woman's Hour: Our Fight for the Right to Vote* (Adapted for Young Readers). New York: Random House Books for Young Readers, 2020.

Zeilinger, Julie. *A Little F'd Up: Why Feminism Is Not a Dirty Word*. New York: Seal Press, 2012.

Social Media Accounts

Want to learn more about fourth-wave feminism? Environmental activism? Girls who code? Follow these activists and world changers on Instagram or Twitter:

@aranyajohar, a slam poet from India who writes about gender equality and education for girls. Yes, please!

@betelhem_dessie, an Ethiopian voice for girls in technology who uses her platform to highlight African tech initiatives

@bodyposipanda, a woman striving for self-love and acceptance for all

@helenagualinga, an Indigenous human rights activist from Ecuador

@nadyaokamoto, an entrepreneur who founded the nonprofit PERIOD at age 16 to help all girls access menstrual products

@thedailyfeminist_education, Julia's organization, which teaches about feminism and activism through weekly themes

@thefemalelead, an account that highlights powerful women and educates on feminist issues

@theworldwithmnr, Canadian twins who are advocates for girls' education in their country of birth, Pakistan

@womensmarchyouth, the youth branch of the worldwide women's marches, with information about feminist events and opportunities for young girls

Mental Health Resources Online

The internet offers a variety of mental health resources and education for young people. Here are some great social media accounts to check out!

@7Cups, a community of listeners who provide free and anonymous emotional support

@activeminds, a student-led initiative that offers education on and prompts conversations about mental health

@browngirltherapy, a place for immigrants and children of immigrants to learn about mental health

@girltrek, an organization that encourages Black people to use healthy coping mechanisms

@iweigh, a place to learn about building confidence and positive body image

@sadgirlsclub, an organization providing resources for women's mental health

@trevorproject, a place where people can learn about pronouns, triggers and mental health resources for LGBT2Q+ youth

Real-Life Mental Health Resources

If you're ever feeling depressed or having suicidal thoughts, reach out for help. Here are some off-line resources designed to support young people.

- **Call 833-456-4566** or **text 45645** for the Canadian suicide prevention hotline.

- **Call 1-800-273-8255** for the American suicide prevention hotline.

- **Text HOME** to **741741** to talk to Crisis Text Line about mental health, stress, school or other problems.

- **Call Kids Help Phone at 1-800-668-6868**.

In an emergency, call 9-1-1 to get help.

ACKNOWLEDGMENTS

Thank you to all those who helped create this book, including Amy Tompkins of Transatlantic Literary Agency, Kirstie Hudson of Orca Book Publishers, illustrator Vivian Rosas, designer Dahlia Yuen and copyeditor Vivian Sinclair. Thank you also to those who provided images and generously answered our many questions, including Katherine White of the University of British Columbia, Johanna Johnson of Peru's La Mini Academia, Emily McQueen of Girl Effect and Julie Zeilinger of *WMC Fbomb*.

—T.K. and J.K.

Thank you to Adelaide and Aishwarya, my Daily Feminist team, for pushing me in my activism and letting me ramble about the intersectional octopus. Thank you to my dog, Coby, for sleeping on my feet while I write, and thank you to my mom, for fixing all my typos in this book. Lastly, thank you for reading. Never underestimate your power to make amazing change!

—J.K.

INDEX

*Page numbers in **bold** indicate an image caption.*

IAN REDD

TANYA LLOYD KYI is the author of more than 25 fiction and nonfiction books for young readers, including *This Is Your Brain on Stereotypes* and *Me and Banksy*. She loves stories about science, history and pop culture, or various combinations of the three. Because Tanya works in the early mornings, while Julia prefers to write late at night, the two communicate mainly through Google Docs...and occasionally at the dinner table. Tanya and Julia live in Vancouver, BC.

IAN REDD

JULIA KYI is a 17-year-old student and activist. Along with her friends Adelaide and Aishwarya, she runs a chapter of Girls Learn International, as well as The Daily Feminist, a workshop series for middle-grade students. You can find the organization on Instagram at @thedailyfeminist_education.

Julia enjoys writing spoken-word poetry and reading sad books. In the future she's planning to complete a social justice degree before applying to law school. She's an avid user of Instagram and TikTok, and a believer in the power of social media to make positive change. She wanted to be part of *Better Connected* because she knows girls can make a difference across the internet, and she was tired of hearing about only the negatives. You can find her reading one of her many library books or telling her mom that teens don't say "YOLO."

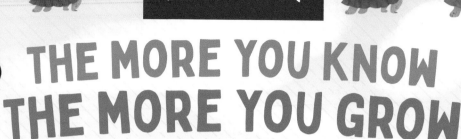

THE MORE YOU KNOW THE MORE YOU GROW

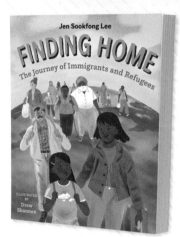

Jen Sookfong Lee

FINDING HOME
The Journey of Immigrants and Refugees

ILLUSTRATED BY Drew Shannon

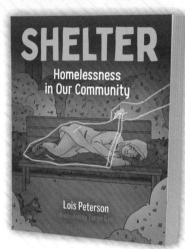

SHELTER
Homelessness in Our Community

Lois Peterson

Illustrated by Taryn Gee

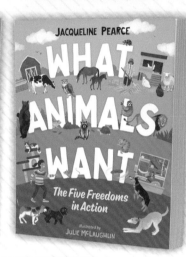

JACQUELINE PEARCE

WHAT ANIMALS WANT
The Five Freedoms in Action

illustrated by JULIE McLAUGHLIN

SAVE NATURAL HABITATS!!

Megan Clendenan
illustrated by Julie McLaughlin

Fresh Air, Clean Water
Our Right to a Healthy Environment

SOLUTIONS not POLLUTION!

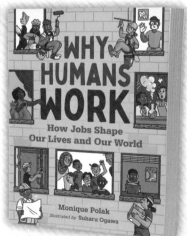

WHY HUMANS WORK
How Jobs Shape Our Lives and Our World

Monique Polak
illustrated by Suharu Ogawa

PETIT

WHAT'S THE BIG IDEA?

The **Orca Think** series introduces us to the issues making headlines in the world today. It encourages us to question, connect and take action for a better future. With those tools we can all become better citizens. Now that's smart thinking!